Devotional Catechism of the Americas of our Catholic Faith

Reverend Father Andrew J. Heintz

This catechism was adapted with permission from the original catechism of the parish of San Pedro in Monsefu, in the Diocese of Chiclayo, Peru.

The cover image is a fresco by Italian artist Luca Giordano, entitled *The Glory of the Spanish Monarchy*, and is located above the main staircase of the Escorial Palace in Madrid.

Table Of Content

THE CATHOLIC CHURCH IS YOUR HOME IN EVERY COUNTRY OF THE WORLD!

PRESENTATION

This catechism, like all the catechisms of our Catholic faith, aims to present an organic and synthetic exposition of the essential and fundamental contents of Catholic doctrine, both on faith and morals, in the light of the Second Vatican Council and the whole of the Church's Tradition. Its principal sources are Sacred Scripture, the Holy Fathers, the Liturgy, and the Magisterium of the Church. It is intended to serve "as a point of reference for catechisms or compendiums to be composed in various countries" (Synod of Bishops 1985, Final Report II, B, a, 4).

All catechisms are intended primarily for those responsible for catechesis: in the first place, for the Bishops, as doctors of the faith and pastors of the Church. It is offered to them as an instrument for carrying out their task of teaching the People of God. Through the Bishops, it is addressed to editors of catechisms, priests, and catechists. It will also be useful reading for all the Christian faithful.

The plan of this catechism is inspired by the great tradition of catechisms, which articulate catechesis around four "pillars": the profession of the baptismal faith (the Symbol), the sacraments of faith, the life of faith (the Commandments), the prayer of the believer (the Lord's Prayer).

This catechism, like all catechisms, is an instrument of the New Evangelization and thus essential in our time as a source of basic education in our faith.

Also, this book is a devotional book that wants to transmit different prayers and "devotions" that serve as a source of our communication with God.

+ The Most Reverend Michael F. Burbidge
Bishop of Arlington

INTRODUCTION

We come from all the countries of the Americas, but we form one family in Christ. We are united by our faith, and we are united by Our Lady of Guadalupe: The Patroness of the Americas.

As human beings, made in the image and likeness of God, we have a great dignity and a great destiny. As we go through life, we must stay close to God and practice our faith so that by keeping God's commandments and doing His will, we may receive our reward of eternal life in Heaven.

This catechism, adapted with permission from the original catechism of St. Peter's Parish in Monsefu, in the Diocese of Chiclayo, Peru, is a brief summary of our Catholic faith, which is designed to help us grow closer to God in our lives of faith, on Earth, so that one day we may enjoy eternal life with God in Heaven.

Reverend Father Andrew J. Heintz

1. I AM A CHRISTIAN

1.- Who is a good Christian?

A good Christian is one who is baptized, believes in Jesus Christ, lives his doctrine, and follows him, accepting all that the Lord instituted.

2.- What should the Christian know?

The Christian should know the Doctrine that Jesus taught us and that is transmitted in a simple way by the Catechism.

3.- What is Catechism?

It is the summary of our faith and a gift of God and the Church to all Christians and people of good will. It is universal because it applies to all the Catholic faithful in any part of the world.

4.- What are the main topics covered in the catechism?

First, what we are to believe or the creed;

Second, what we should celebrate or the liturgy (the Sacraments);

Third, how we are to live or the commandments, and

Fourth, how we should pray or the Lord's Prayer and principal prayers.

PART ONE: PROFESSION OF FAITH

I believe in God, the Father almighty, Creator of heaven and earth. I believe in Jesus Christ, his only Son, our Lord, who was conceived by the power and grace of the Holy Spirit, was born of the Virgin Mary, suffered under Pontius Pilate, was crucified, died and was buried, descended into hell, on the third day rose again from the dead, ascended into heaven, and is seated at the right hand of God, the Father almighty. From there, he will come to judge the living and the dead. I believe in the Holy Spirit, the holy catholic Church, the communion of saints, the forgiveness of sins, the resurrection of the body, and the life everlasting. Amen.

CHAPTER I: I BELIEVE - WE BELIEVE

2. MAN HAS THE ABILITY TO KNOW GOD:

"The desire for God is inscribed in man's heart, because man is created by God and for God; ... and only in God will man find the truth and the happiness that he never ceases to seek" (CCC 27).

Smoke   = Fire
Fire   = Cause
Creation= Creator

In nature we can recognize the traces of God

<u>Our knowledge of God</u>

Movement in the world requires a prime mover

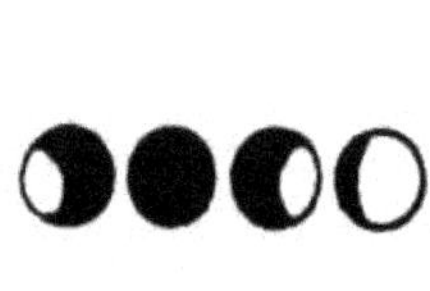 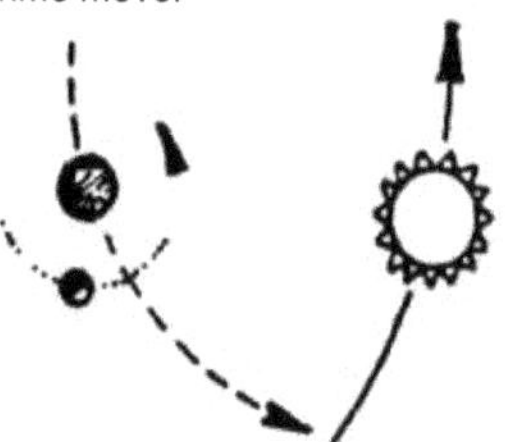 

Becoming and ceasing to be claim eternal being

 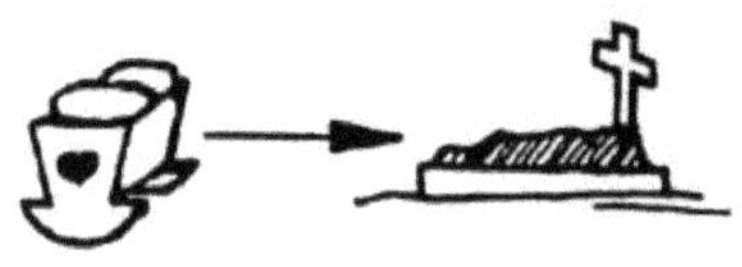

The admirable order cries out for a wise Creator

5.- What does it mean to believe?
Belief is the response of faith on the part of man to God, who has revealed himself; it is the confidence that God exists and exists for all people, knows them, and loves them. Man, being a religious being by nature and vocation, is made to love and live in friendship with his creator, so no one, no matter how atheist he may consider himself, can eliminate God from his life.

6.- Why did God want to reveal himself to man?
Because he wanted to show His great love.

7.- What does it mean to reveal?
That God communicates or makes known to man His divine life and will through actions and words since creation throughout human history.

8.- What are the most important historical stages of this revelation?
God revealed himself at the beginning of history to our first parents, then to Noah, Abraham, and Moses, and then to the priests and prophets. And finally the life and work of Jesus Christ is the fullness of revelation.

9.- How did the apostles transmit God's revelation to us?
Orally and in writing, under the action of the Holy Spirit. In this way, the only deposit of the Faith is constituted.

10.- What do we mean by writing?
It is the Holy Scripture (BIBLE), which is the Word of God.

11.- What do we mean by orally?
It is the Tradition of the Church, which transmits the Word of God in its entirety to all peoples, from Jesus to his apostles and these to their successors (The Church).

12.- Who is responsible for interpreting God's revelation?

To the Magisterium of the Church, that is, to the Pope and the bishops in communion with him.

3. HOLY SCRIPTURE: "When we read the Bible, it is God who speaks to us through it" (Dt. 4:10)

The sources of revelation

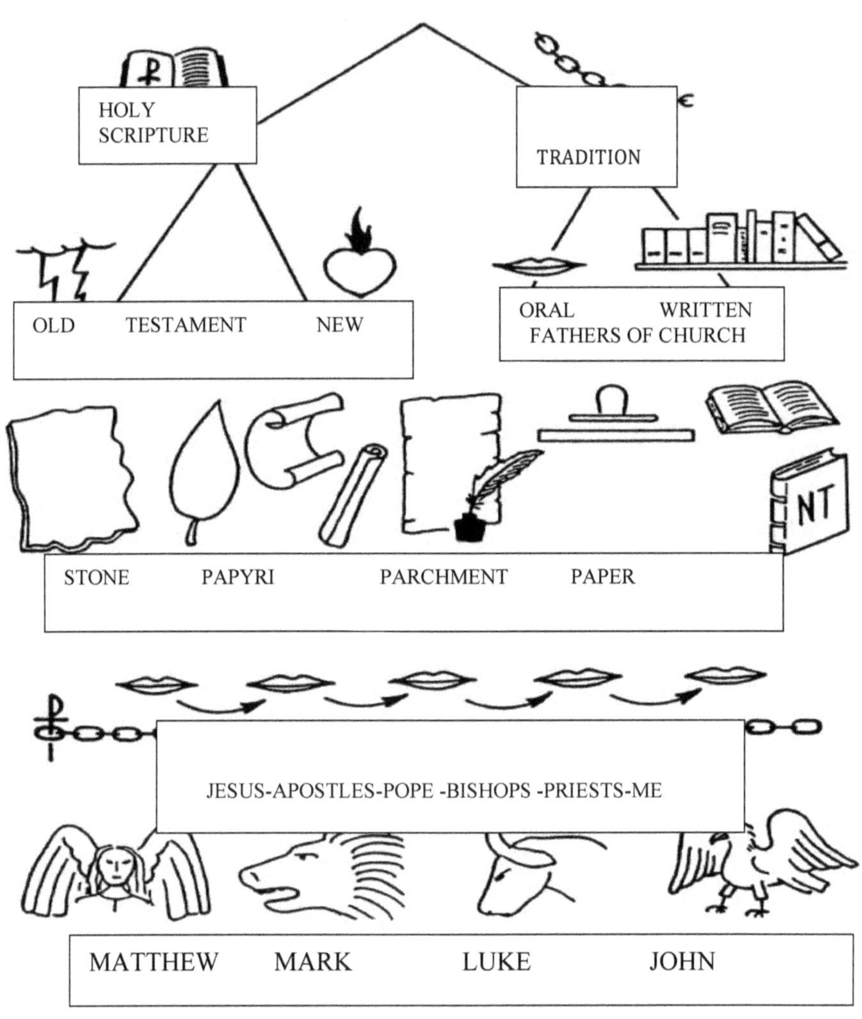

Early meaning of the symbols of the Evangelists: man = incarnation, bull = crucifixion, lion = resurrection, eagle = ascension of Christ.

13.- What is Holy Scripture?

It is the Word of God written by the inspiration of the Holy Spirit and found in the set of books we call the Bible.

14.- Who is the author of Holy Scripture?

The principal Author of the Holy Scripture is God, and it was written by chosen men inspired by the Holy Spirit (secondary authors) (2 Tim. 3:16).

15.- What does Holy Scripture teach?

Holy Scripture teaches without error the truth of our salvation.

16.- How many books does Holy Scripture consist of?

It consists of seventy-three books (73): forty-six (46) of the Old Testament and twenty-seven (27) of the New Testament.

4. MAN'S ANSWER TO GOD: The Catholic Faith is a Gift that God has given us

17.- What is faith?

Faith is the trust and personal acceptance of the intelligence and will of the divine revelation.

Faith is a supernatural gift because in order to believe, man needs divine help.

18.- What does faith give us?

Faith gives us the power to believe in God and to know the truths revealed by Him in order to correspond to His love.

OUR PARISH AND
OUR CHURCH IS
FOR US A
HOUSE OF GOD AND GATEWAY TO HEAVEN

THE PARISH IS MY HOME

I belong to the Diocese of:_______________________________________

My Bishop's name is:____

My Parish is called:____

The priests are called:____

I was baptized on:_______________/________________/ 20

CHAPTER II: TWELVE ARTICLES OF THE CREED

5. **FIRST ARTICLE: "I believe in God, the Father Almighty, Creator of heaven and earth".**

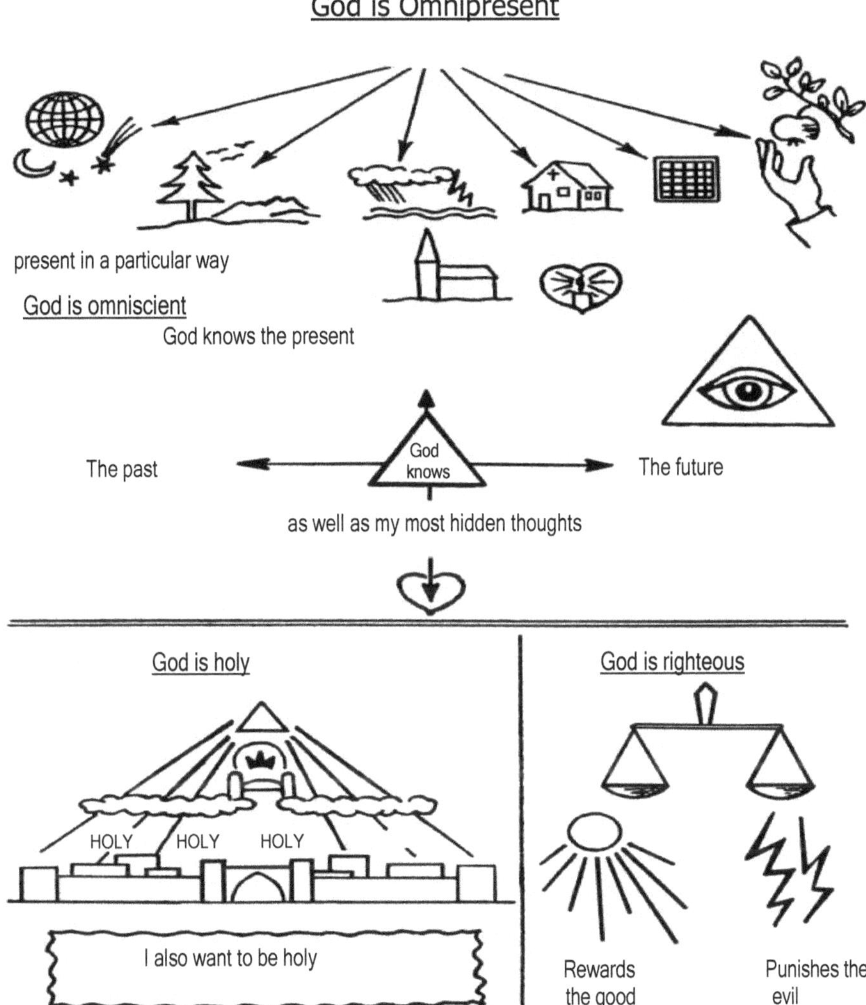

19.- Who is God?
God is our Father who is in heaven, on earth, and in every place, the Beginning and the End of all things. Who rewards the good and punishes the wicked.

20.- What are the main attributes of God?
The God of Christians is one God; he is also a living, merciful, and gracious God; he is above all Truth and Love.

21.- Does God see everything?
God sees everything: past, present, and future, and even our most hidden thoughts.

6. THE BLESSED TRINITY: Our entire faith is Trinitarian (Mt. 28:19)

22.- What is the central mystery of our faith?
The central mystery of our faith is the mystery of the Holy Trinity.

23.- Who is the Holy Trinity?
He is the same Father, Son, and Holy Spirit, three distinct persons in one true God.

24.- What is it that introduces us to the mystery and life of the Trinity?
The grace of Baptism which is given to us in the name of the Father and of the Son, and of the Holy Spirit.

25.- In summary, what is the Catholic faith in the Trinity?
The Catholic faith is this: we believe and venerate one God in three distinct persons with equal glory and eternal majesty.

7. GOD HAS CREATED EVERYTHING: To create is to make something good out of nothing (Gen. 1:10-25).

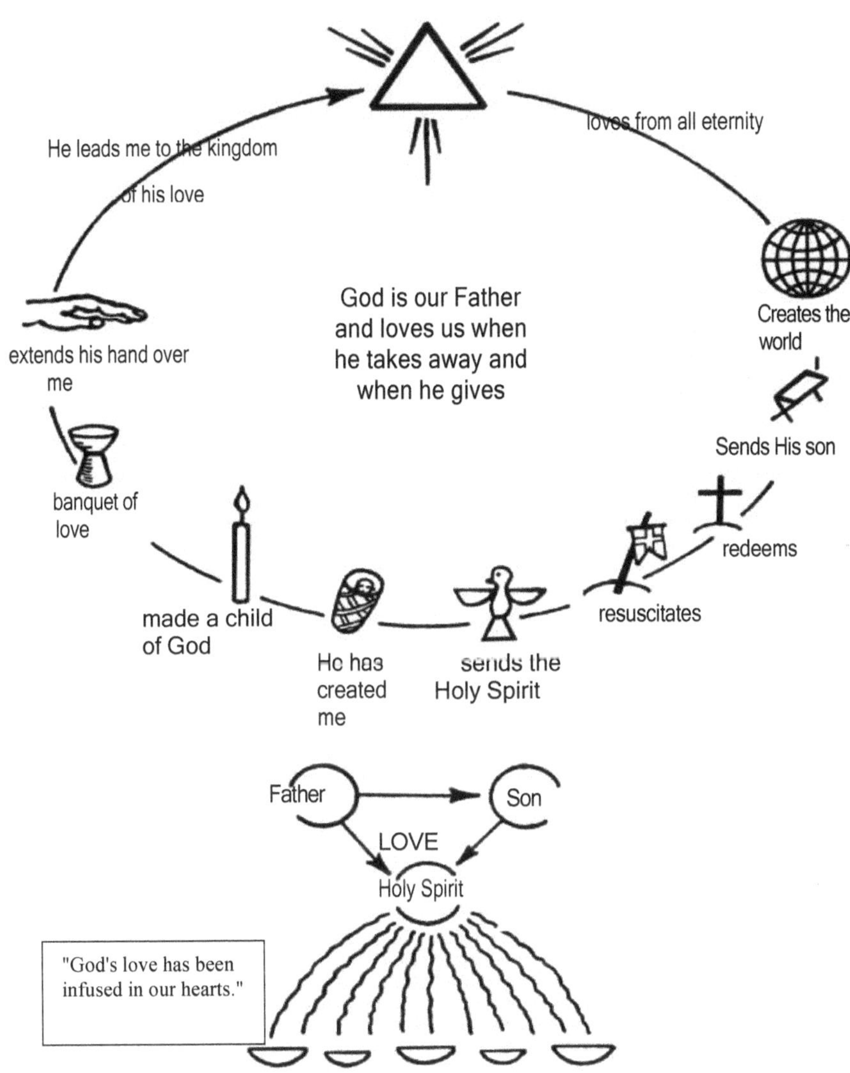

26.- What does it mean that God is Almighty?
It means that nothing is impossible for Him. He can do everything.

27.- How does God manifest his Omnipotence?
God manifests his Omnipotence by creating us, forgiving our sins, and sanctifying us with his grace.

28.- What is the purpose of the creation of the world?
The purpose of the creation of the world is to manifest and communicate the glory of God.

29.- To whom is the work of creation primarily attributed?
The work of creation is attributed to God the Father.

30.- What do we call Divine Providence?
We call divine providence the dispositions by which God, with wisdom and love, leads creation to its perfection. Therefore, God does not abandon what he has made but takes care of it and wants everything to have a good end.

31.- Then why does evil and death exist?
There is evil and death because of the envy of the Devil, who is evil and a liar, and because of the sin of our first parents.

32.- What does it mean that God is the creator of heaven and earth?
It means that God has created everything that exists out of nothing: the angels, the world, and man. Man can be called an inventor, discoverer, builder, but only God the Creator.

8. INVISIBLE CREATURES: We cannot see them, but they exist

33.- Who are the angels?
Angels are spiritual creatures endowed with intelligence and will.

34.- What is the mission of the angels?
The mission of the angels is to glorify God without ceasing and to help men to live according to God.

35.- Who is the guardian angel?
The Guardian Angel or Guardian Angel is the one that God gives to each one of us to protect us and help us reach heaven. We should all invoke him daily with devotion.

PRAYER
(Pray every day and whenever you need his help.
He will guide you on the right path)
Angel of my guardian, sweet companion, do not forsake me,
night or day, do not leave me alone or I would lose my way.
Amen.

9. THE VISIBLE CREATURES: Everything that surrounds us and mankind as the ultimate work (Ps. 8:3-8)

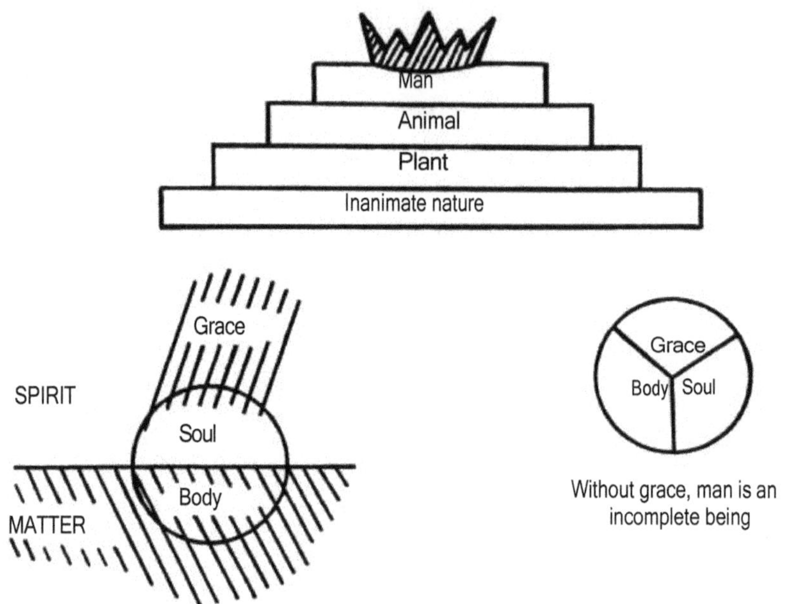

Without grace, man is an incomplete being

Man is the image and likeness of God

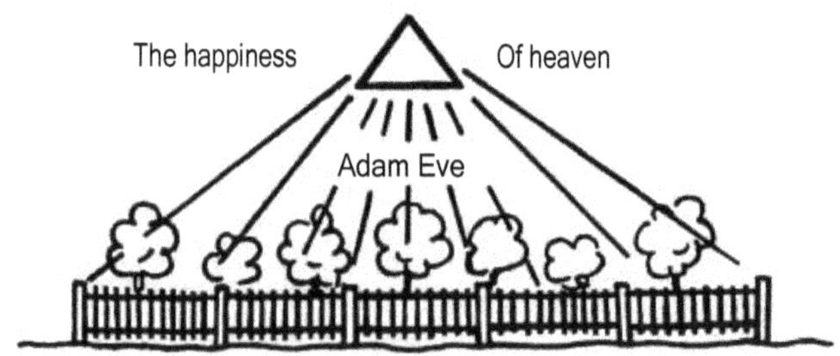

for the body: imprint of God
by the soul: image of God
by grace: likeness of God

The happiness of the first parents?

36.- What does it mean that God has created the world?
It means that He has brought out of nothing all nature and all beings that exist.

37.- Is there a hierarchy in creation?
Yes, and man is the summit of all creation because only he can know and love God.

38.- How did God create man?
Man has been created in the image and likeness of God, with clay representing the body and with the breath of God representing the soul; he is rational, free, responsible, and capable of knowing and loving to serve Him in this life and then to enjoy Him in heaven.

39.- What is the soul like?
The soul is spiritual and immortal, endowed with intelligence and will, created directly by God.

40.- How did God create human beings?
He created man and woman in equality of nature and in communion of persons. God does not want male chauvinism or family violence because we are all equal.

(Gen. 2:18-24).

Think that...

No one is unaware that they have to die here on earth. We are only passing through.
The important thing for the one who is passing through is to reach the goal: to attain eternal happiness, which is not to be found on earth.
It is up to you to be happy here, as far as possible, and to secure your happiness forever.
If you try hard, you can be eternally unhappy, separated from God.
God loves you very much, he wants you to be eternally happy, he wants you to be saved. Trust in him completely.
If you condemn yourself, you have failed in the most important business of your existence.

10. ORIGINAL SIN: The cause of all evils

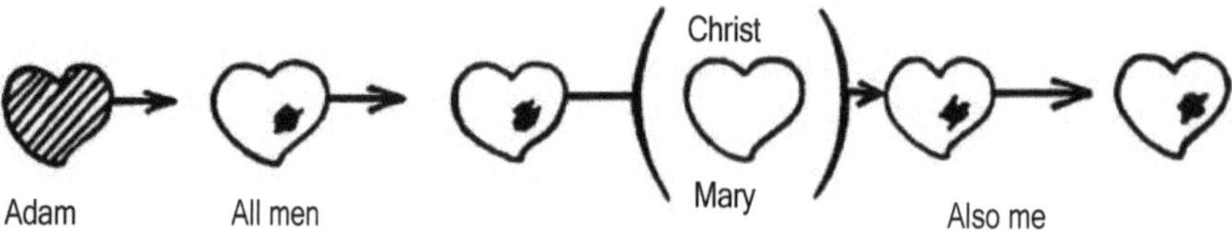

<u>Consequences of original sin</u>

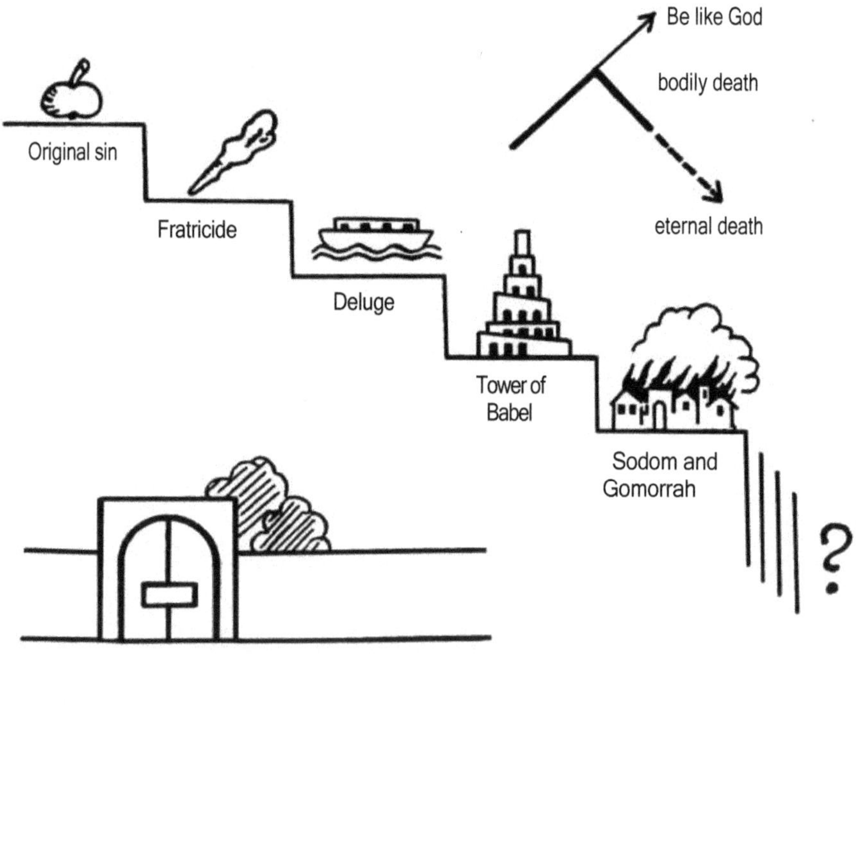

41.- Who was the first creature to sin?
The first creature to sin was the devil.

42.- In what did the sin of the first man consist?
In that, abusing his freedom, he rose up against God and preferred himself to God.

43.- What was the consequence for the first man of this first sin?
Adam lost, for himself and for all his male and female descendants, the original holiness and righteousness he had received from God.

44.- What consequences did original sin bring us?
Our human nature was weakened in its strength, subjected to ignorance, suffering, and the dominion of death, and inclined to sin.

45.- Did God abandon man after his fall?
No, he did not abandon him but announced to him in a mysterious way the victory over evil and the emergence from his fall (Gen. 3:15).

46.- What did this announcement of victory over evil consist of?
In the proclamation of the Good News of Jesus Christ, Son of God.

Christ
Olive branch
Abel
rainbow
Ark (= Church)
Old Alliance
1 2 3
4 5 6 7 8 9 10
Melchizedek
Rock water
Manna
Bronze snake
Jonah
JOHN
is his name
From the roots
sprouts a shoot

11. SECOND ARTICLE: "I believe in Jesus Christ, his only Son, our Lord"

47.- What does "Jesus" mean?
Jesus means "God saves."

48.- What does the name of Christ mean?
It means "Messiah," which means "Anointed" by the Holy Spirit.

49.- Who is Jesus Christ?
Jesus Christ is the Son of God, made man who was born of the Virgin Mary, died on the cross to save all men, and rose again on the third day.

12. THIRD ARTICLE: "Jesus Christ was conceived by the work and grace of the Holy Spirit and was born of the Virgin Mary."

50.- What is Incarnation?
The Incarnation is the mystery of the union of the divine nature and the human nature in the one person of God the Son.

51.- How did the Incarnation of the Son of God take place?
It was accomplished by the Holy Spirit forming, from the purest womb of the Virgin Mary, a perfect body and creating a most noble soul that united to that body and soul the Son of God, without ceasing to be, became man.

52.- Why did the Son of God become man?

He became man to save us and reconcile us with God.

53.- Are the two natures, divine and human, confused in Jesus Christ?
No, they are not confused but are united in the one Person of the Son
of God. That is, Jesus Christ is true God and true man in the unity of a
single person who is divine.

13. OUR MOTHER IN HEAVEN:
   Immaculate Virgin Mary

54.- Who is the Blessed Virgin Mary?
She is the Lady full of graces and virtues, conceived without original sin,
who is the Mother of God and our mother and is in heaven, body, and
soul.

55.- How did God prepare Mary for this vocation?
He prepared her by preserving her from original sin and filling her with
every grace and blessing. Our Lady was sinless because of her holiness
and her mission.

56.- What are the main privileges that God granted to Saint Mary?
They are four: Her immaculate conception (she had no original sin), her
perpetual virginity (virgin before, during, and after childbirth), her divine
Maternity (Mother of Jesus who is God), and her assumption body and
soul into heaven (at the throne of God she intercedes for us).

57.- How did the Virgin Mary collaborate in the work of salvation?
She collaborated with her faith and obedience. That is why she occupies
the place of co-redeemer (collaborator) of Salvation. Today, she
continues to intercede for us, her children.

14. JESUS LIVES AMONG US: He is like us in His humanity, but perfect

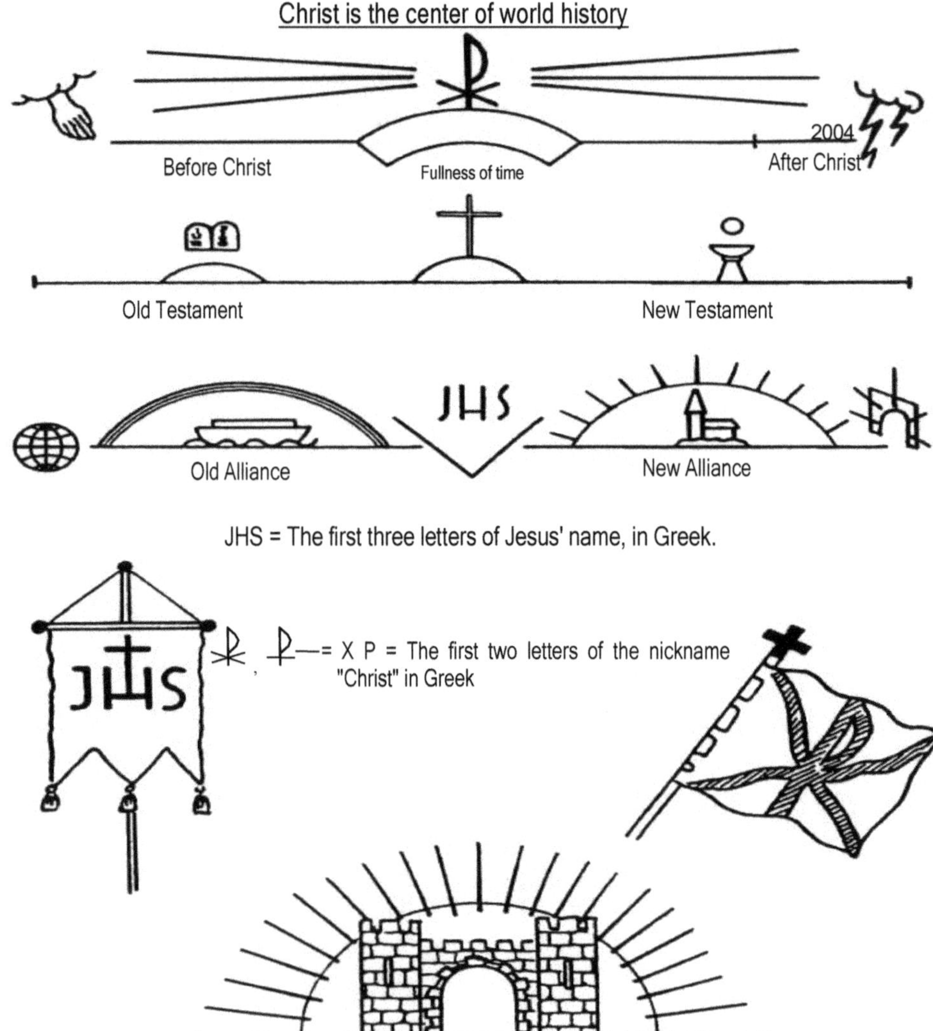

Childhood: Bethlehem.

58.- What does Christ's earthly life teach us?
It teaches us all that Jesus did, said, and suffered to restore us to friendship with God.

59.- What should be our attitude towards the life and teachings of Jesus?
We must imitate his example and follow his teaching because he is a perfect man.

60.- What are the main mysteries of Jesus' infancy?
The birth in Bethlehem, the **circumcision** in the temple of Jerusalem, the **Epiphany,** which was the adoration of the Magi, the **presentation** of Jesus in the temple, and **the flight to Egypt** because Herod wanted to kill him.

THE WORST IGNORANCE

+
It is the one that refers to religion, because only true happiness and peaceful and just coexistence among men is assured.
It is necessary to know and practice the most basic truths of the faith and not to neglect the most elementary prayers of the Christian.
The de-Christianization of society, the secularization of the environment is what explains so much of today's evils.
When the Christian lives his faith, he spreads it only by his presence. He should also, as far as possible, be able to give an explanation of what he believes. Often the environment does not help and one must go against the current.

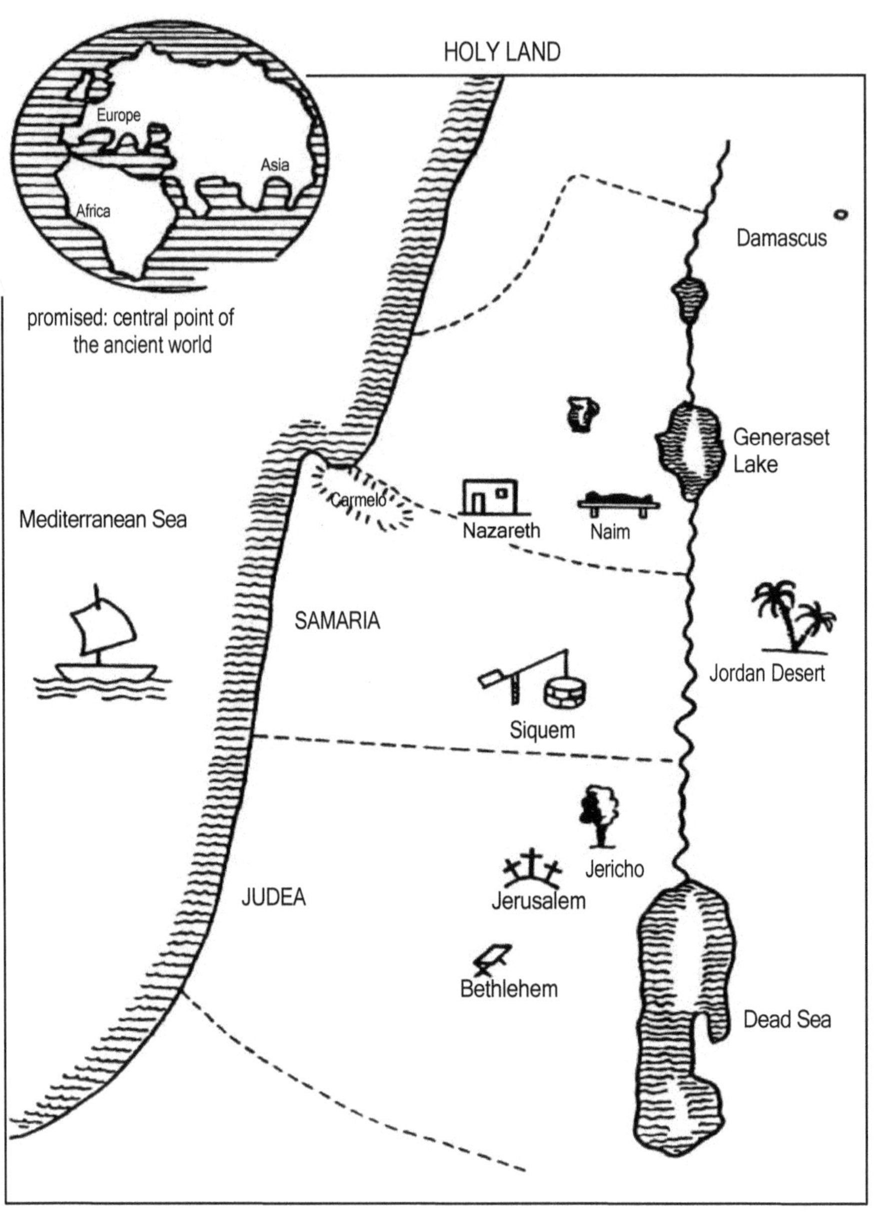

HOLY LAND
Europe
Asia
Africa
promised: central point of
the ancient world
Damascus
Mediterranean Sea
Generaset
Lake
Carmelo
Nazareth
Naim
SAMARIA
Jordan Desert
Siquem
Jericho
Jerusalem
JUDEA
Bethlehem
Dead Sea

Hidden Life: Nazareth

61.- What are the main mysteries of the hidden life of Jesus?
There are two: the daily life of work, prayer, and obedience in Nazareth and the event of Jesus being lost and found in the Temple.

62.- What do these moments in the life of Jesus teach us?
They teach us to be saints in our daily family and work life, no matter how simple it is worthy in the eyes of God.

Jesus, Our Master

When Jesus had finished speaking the people marveled at the doctrine: Mt. 7:28

His words are hard! Who can follow them? Jn. 6:60

Learn from me, for I am meek and humble of heart: Mt. 11:29

In him are the treasures of wisdom hidden: Col. 2:3

Jesus went through all the towns teaching the Good News: Mt. 9:35

They should not expect people to call them teachers: Mt. 23:8

You call me Master and Lord, because I am: Jn. 13:3

No man ever spoke like this: Jn. 7:46

My teaching is not mine, but that of the one who sent me: Jn. 7:16

Even though the scriptures speak of me, you do not want to come: Jn. 7:39

Public Life: Palestine (Lk. 3:23)

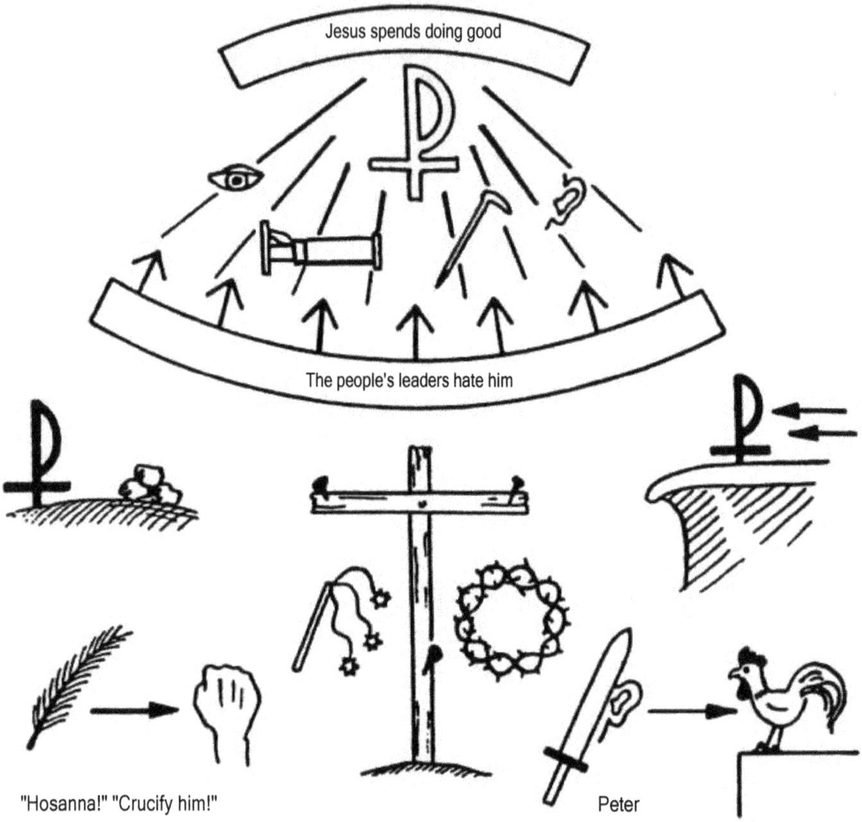

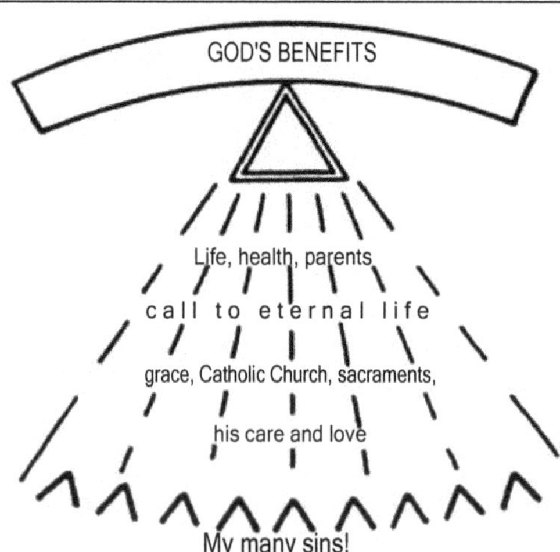

"My people, what have I done to you, answer me!"

63.- What are the main mysteries of Jesus' public life?
They are the baptism (in the Jordan) and the temptations (in the desert), the preaching of the Kingdom of God (throughout the Holy Land) and the miracles, the transfiguration (on Mount Tabor, he showed his divinity to the apostles) and the triumphal entry into Jerusalem (Palm Sunday).

64.- What do we learn from His Baptism?
We learn total acceptance of the Father's Will for the salvation of mankind.

65.- What does Jesus teach us through His temptations?
He teaches us to overcome the devil with obedience to the Will of God.

66.- What does Jesus teach us through His preaching and miracles?
He teaches us that the Kingdom of God is a mystery, that it is already present and active among men, and that we are all called to enter it, regardless of social condition, culture, and even less of race. Jesus became a man for all of us.

Meditate brother/sister

This book will help you to be a good Christian and to save yourself, read it with interest, meditate on it with affection.

In his merciful love, God has gone so far as to give his Son to death so that you may be saved.

It is easy to be a good Christian if you seek to deal with God: if you work often.

Plants dry up if they are not watered; the soul dies of anemia if it is not nourished by prayer.

15. FOURTH ARTICLE: "He suffered under Pontius Pilate, was crucified, died, and was buried"

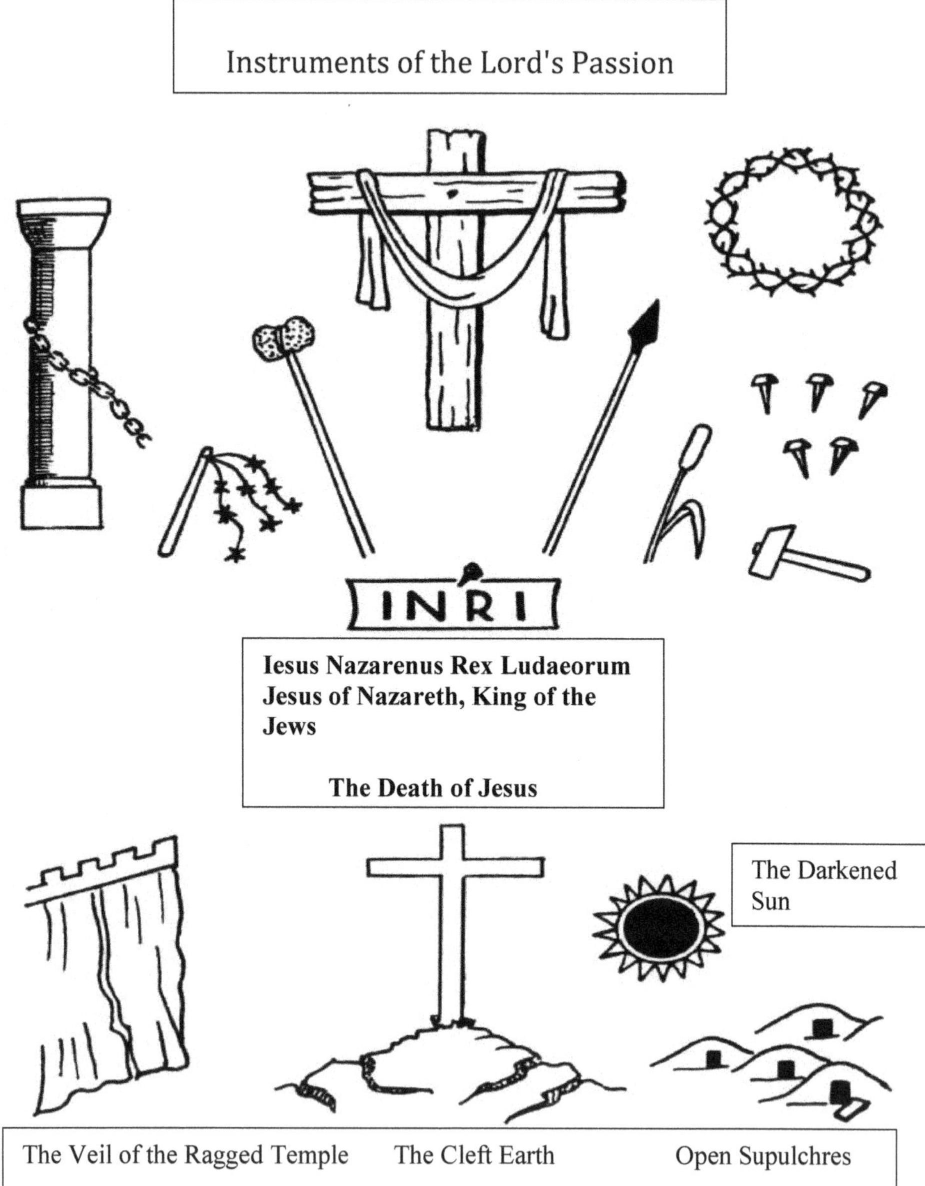

67.- Why was he condemned to death by the Jewish authorities?
Because he seemed to act against what was most sacred to the Chosen People: the Law, the Temple, and Yahweh, the only God, Jesus was seen as an impostor or enemy.

68.- Why did Christ die on the cross?
Christ died on the cross for our sins, according to the Scriptures. He paid with his blood the punishment that should have fallen on us.

69.- What effect did Christ's death have?
The redemption and atonement of the whole human race.

<u>IN CRITICAL SITUATIONS</u>
<u>TURN TO THE BIBLE FOR LIGHT</u> ...

- When you are afraid: Read Psalms 121 and 91

- When you are very low: Psalms 77 and 88

- When things go wrong: Psalm 37 and Mt. 8

- When you are sick: Psalms 6 and 39 and Ecclesiasticus 38

- When you are worried: Psalm 149 and Mt. 7

- When you are afraid of evil powers: Psalm 27

- When a loved one dies, and grief overcomes you: 1 Thessalonians 4: 13-18

- When you have sinned grievously: Psalm 51; Lk. 15

- When you are tempted by sin: Mt. 4: 1-10

16. FIFTH ARTICLE: "He descended into hell, on the third day he rose again from the dead"

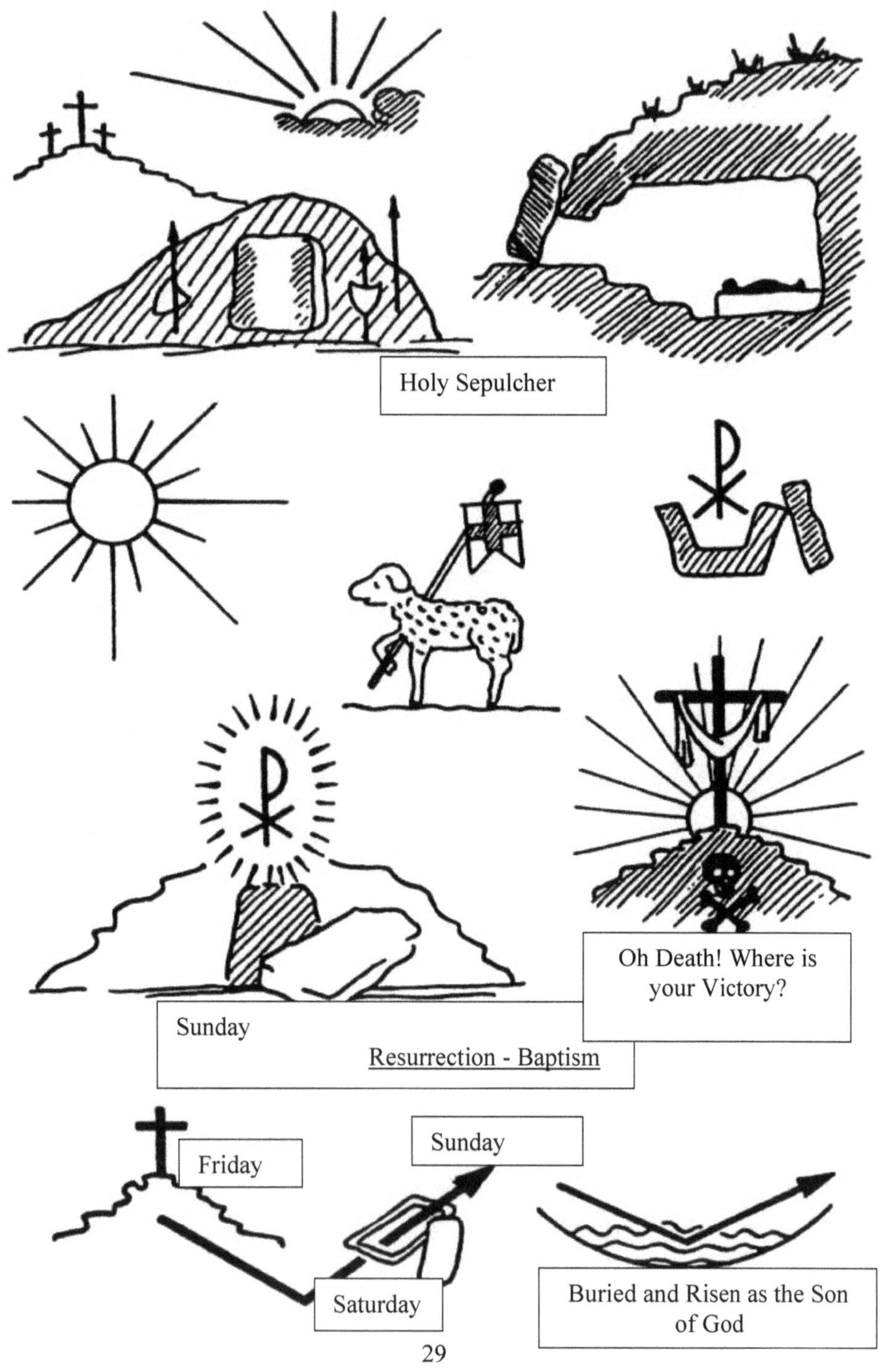

29

70.- What does it mean that Jesus descended into hell?
It means that after the Lord's death, his soul united to his divinity, went to meet the holy souls who awaited his coming in the limbo of the just, to announce redemption to them and take them to heaven.

Resurrection: Sunday

71.- When did Jesus Christ rise from the dead?
Jesus Christ rose from the grave on the third day after his death, Sunday.

72.- What signs bear historical witness to the Resurrection of Jesus?
The empty tomb and the apparitions of Jesus to his disciples for forty (40) days.

73.- What effects did the Resurrection of Christ produce?
It produced several effects: 1st: it confirmed all that Christ did and taught. 2nd, it also confirmed his divinity. And 3rd, it opened for us the entrance to heaven in friendship with God.

17. SIXTH ARTICLE: "He ascended into heaven and is seated at the right hand of God the Father Almighty."

Ascension: With his glorious body

74.- When did Jesus ascend to heaven?
He ascended forty days after his resurrection, after instructing his disciples about the Church.

75.- What does it mean that he is seated at the right hand of God?
It means that Christ has inaugurated the Kingdom of God, toward which we march, hoping to live eternally with Him. It also means that as Father, He is God.

76.- What is Jesus Christ doing for us in heaven?
He intercedes unceasingly for us before His Father God.

18. SEVENTH ARTICLE: "From there, he will come to judge the living and the dead"

JESUS WILL COME AGAIN: Eschatology

77.- What happens in the time between the Ascension and the second coming of Christ?
The Church begins and grows the Kingdom of Christ on earth, allowing herself to be guided by the Spirit, bearing witness and fighting against evil.

78.- When will the second coming of Christ be?
At a particular moment in history, known only to God.

79.- What will the judgment of Christ consist of?
It will consist of revealing the secret of every heart and repaying every man according to his deeds.

Thoughts

Meditate on it often: I am a Catholic, a child of Christ's Church! He has made me to be born in a home of "His", without any merit on my part - how much I owe You, my God!
How much I owe you, my God! (Forge 16)

To guard holy purity, cleanliness of life, you must love and practice daily mortification.(Forge 316)

What immutable joy it gives you to have surrendered yourself to God!

And how anxious you must be, and how anxious you must be that all may participate in your joy! (Furrow 88)

Serenity, audacity! Disrupt with these virtues the fifth column of the lukewarm, of the frightened, of the traitors (Furrow 112).

19. EIGHTH ARTICLE: "I believe in the Holy Spirit" "The great unknown" (Jn. 14: 16-17)

80.- Who is the Holy Spirit?
He is the third person of the Blessed Trinity, who, with the Father and the Son, receives the same adoration and glory because he proceeds from the love of both.

81.- What is the mission of the Holy Spirit?
To make Christ known, the visible image of the invisible God. Already from the beginning of creation, he was revealing himself.

82.- What symbols does Scripture use to speak of the Holy Spirit?
It uses the symbols of water, anointing, and fire, and mainly the dove.

83.- When did the work of the Holy Spirit reach its fullness?
When the Holy Spirit performed in Mary the conception of the Son of God.

84.- When did the Holy Spirit become present in the Church?
When Christ, on the day of Pentecost, communicated the Holy Spirit to the disciples.

85.- What and what are the gifts of the Holy Spirit?
They are permanent dispositions, infused by God, that make man docile to follow the impulses of the Holy Spirit and are seven: Wisdom, Understanding, Counsel, Fortitude, Knowledge, Piety and Fear of God.

20. NINTH ARTICLE: "I believe in the Holy Catholic Church" (1 Cor. 12: 27-30)

The supreme power of Saint Peter

86.- What does the word "Church" mean?"
It means the community of believers who, as the baptized people of God, are scattered throughout the world and who live by the Word and the Body of Christ. These people gather around one Lord, one faith, one baptism.

87.- Who founded the Church?
Jesus Christ, with the proclamation of the Kingdom of God through his redemptive death on the cross and his Resurrection.

88.- How did Jesus begin the foundation of the Church?
Jesus began the foundation with the preaching of the Kingdom of God, calling from among the disciples who followed him the twelve Apostles and appointing Peter head of them all.

89.- Why do we say that the Church is a mystery?
Because it is at once visible and spiritual, human and divine, a hierarchical society and the Mystical Body of Christ.

90.- What is the mission of the Church?
It is the same as that of Jesus Christ: to carry out God's saving plan for mankind.

91.- What are the distinguishing marks of the true Church?
That it is One, Holy, Catholic, and Apostolic.

ONE
Doctrine in the Sacraments and the Supreme Head

HOLY
Sanctified by Christ

CATHOLIC
To all nations of the world

APOSTOLIC
It goes back to the Apostles

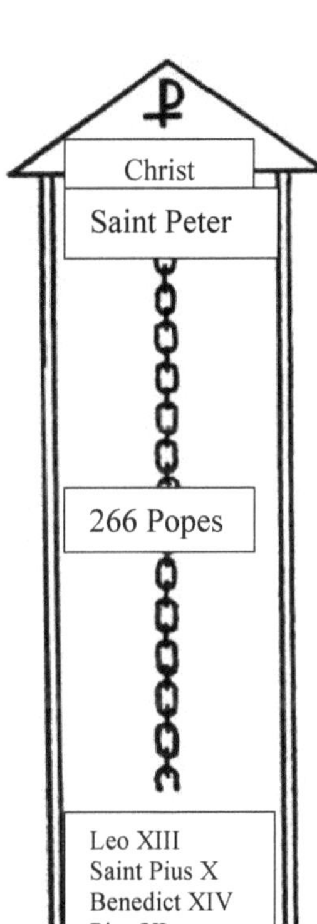

2x2=3
=5
=3.5
=4
=5.5

Example taken from arithmetic to demonstrate that there is only one true church and that the others are more or less false.

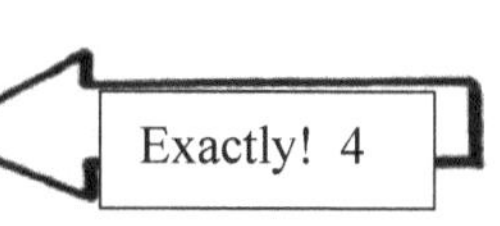

92.- Why do we say it is One?
Because it has one Lord who confesses one faith and one baptism and forms one Body in one Spirit.

93.- Why do we say it is Holy?
For God, its author is holy; Christ, its spouse, gave himself for it to sanctify it, and the Holy Spirit vivifies it.

94.- Are all Christians called to holiness?
Yes, although we are sinners, all Christians are called to holiness, each in his or her own way.

95.- Why do we say that the Church is Catholic?
It is catholic because it proclaims the totality of the faith, possesses all the means of salvation, is sent to all men, and embraces all times.

96.- Why do we say that the Church is Apostolic?
Because it is built on the apostles and is governed by their successors: the Pope and the bishops.

21. THE FAITHFUL: THE HIERARCHY, THE LAITY, AND THOSE IN CONSECRATED LIFE (1 Pe. 5: 1-4)

97.- Who are the faithful Christians?
The Christian faithful is those who, incorporated into Christ by baptism, are integrated into the people of God and are made sharers in their own way in the priestly, prophetic, and kingly function of Christ to carry out his mission of the Church in the world.

98.- Are all the faithful called to holiness and apostolate?
Yes, all are called to holiness and apostolate, whatever their condition, by the very fact of having received Baptism and Confirmation.

99.- Who is the supreme Pastor and visible head of the Church?
The Supreme Shepherd and invisible Head of the Church is Jesus Christ.

100.- Who is the Pope?

The Pope is the successor of St. Peter, the Vicar of Christ on earth and visible head of the Church, who enjoys supreme, full, immediate, and universal power over the whole Church.

101.- Who are the Bishops?

They are the successors of the apostles and the visible foundation of unity in their particular churches.

102.- Who are the priests?

Priests or presbyters are those who, by priestly ordination, participate sacramentally in the priesthood of Christ and cooperate with the Bishop in preaching the Gospel, administering the sacraments, and bringing to God the faithful entrusted to them, for example, in a parish.

103.- Who are the lay faithful?

Christians are called to bear witness to Christ in the world, to be saints by virtue of their participation in the universal priesthood, wherever they find themselves in their families, parishes, at work or with their friends.

104.- Can the laity be called to collaborate with pastors in the service of their Church?

Yes, they can be called to collaborate in very diverse ministries, according to the graces and charisms that the Lord gives them, for example, as catechists, members of a movement, parish group... or of the promise.

105.- What is meant by consecrated life?

It is the way of life of those Christians who profess the evangelical counsels of poverty, chastity, and obedience in a state of life recognized by the Church in order to follow Jesus Christ more closely and dedicate themselves entirely to the good of mankind.

22. TENTH ARTICLE: "I believe in the communion of Saints" (1 Cor. 12: 26-27)

106.- What does "communion of saints" mean?

Two things: 1st, it means the communion of believers in spiritual goods, especially the Eucharist, and 2nd, the communion of the pilgrim Church with the saints in heaven (Church triumphant) and with all the faithful departed.

23. ELEVENTH ARTICLE: "I believe in the forgiveness of sins and the resurrection of the body" (1 Cor. 15: 12-14)

107.- Who entrusted the apostles with the power to forgive sins?
Jesus Christ entrusted it to them, when He said: "Receive the Holy Spirit and those who forgive sins are forgiven" (Jn. 20: 22-23).

108.- How are our sins forgiven?
Mainly through the sacrament of baptism and the sacrament of Penance.

109.- What does the resurrection of the flesh mean?
It means that God in his omnipotence, will give our bodies incorruptible life, uniting them to our souls by virtue of Christ's Resurrection.

110.- Why do we believe in the resurrection of the flesh?
By the testimony of Christ himself, dead and risen from the dead.

111.- What is death?
It is the separation of soul and body, a consequence of original sin.

112.- What is the meaning of Christian death?
Death is the end of man's earthly pilgrimage, the end of the time of grace that God offers him to fulfill his life according to the divine plan and to decide his ultimate destiny.

24. TWELFTH ARTICLE: "I believe in eternal life. Amen."
(Heb. 9:27)

113.- What happens after death?
Each man is judged by Christ in a particular judgment and is given a reward or punishment according to his works.

114.- Who goes to heaven?
Those who die in grace and friendship with God are perfectly purified from all sin.

115.- What is heaven?
It is the communion of life and love with God, the Virgin Mary, the angels, and the saints in a definitive state of happiness.

116.- Who goes to purgatory?
Those who die in grace and friendship with God but imperfectly purified.

117.- What is purgatory?
Purgatory is the purification after death in order to obtain the holiness necessary to definitively enjoy God.

118.- Who goes to hell?
Those who voluntarily and freely reject God and persist in their rejection to the end.

119.- What is hell?
It is the eternal separation from God of those who die in grave sin against God, against their neighbor, or against themselves. It is the condemnation by eternal fire with the suffering of all evil without any mixture of good because there is only loneliness and weeping.

120.- What is the final judgment?
It is the time when all men, at the end of time, will give an account to God for their own actions before the judgment seat of Jesus Christ, King of the Universe.

PART TWO: THE CELEBRATION OF THE CHRISTIAN MYSTERY

"Church Liturgy"

121.- What is liturgy?

The liturgy is the set of actions (celebration of rites, gestures, and symbols) by which Christ, Redeemer, and High Priest continue in the Church, with her and through her, the work of our Redemption.

<table>
<tr><td colspan="1" align="center">LITURGICAL TIMES</td></tr>
<tr><td>

1. **ADVENT**: (Purple) It is four weeks of waiting and preparation for the second coming of the Lord, but above all it is the preparation for the coming of the Lord at Christmas.
2. **CHRISTMAS**: (White) Which runs from December 25 until the Sunday after the Epiphany, January 6. We remember the mystery of the birth of Jesus.
3. **LENT**: (Purple) It is the forty days of preparation for the Easter of Resurrection. It begins with Ash Wednesday. It is a time for a greater life of prayer, sacrifice and almsgiving.
4. **EASTER TRIDUUM**:(White) is the culmination of the whole liturgical year because it celebrates the victory of Christ over sin and death and therefore we celebrate the passion, death and resurrection of the Lord.
5. **EASTER**:(White)It is the fifty days of happiness in which the victory of Jesus is celebrated. It lasts until the feast of Pentecost.
6. **ORDINARY TIME**: Covers the rest of the liturgical year and the longest. We celebrate the Lord's Day when we are all obliged to attend Mass. It is composed of 34 weeks.

</td></tr>
</table>

CHAPTER I: SACRAMENTAL ECONOMY

122.- How does Christ continue the work of His redemption?

He continues it primarily through the sacraments and rites of the Church.

25. THE SEVEN SACRAMENTS: "Accompany the Christian's Life".

(1 Cor. 11:26; 15:28)

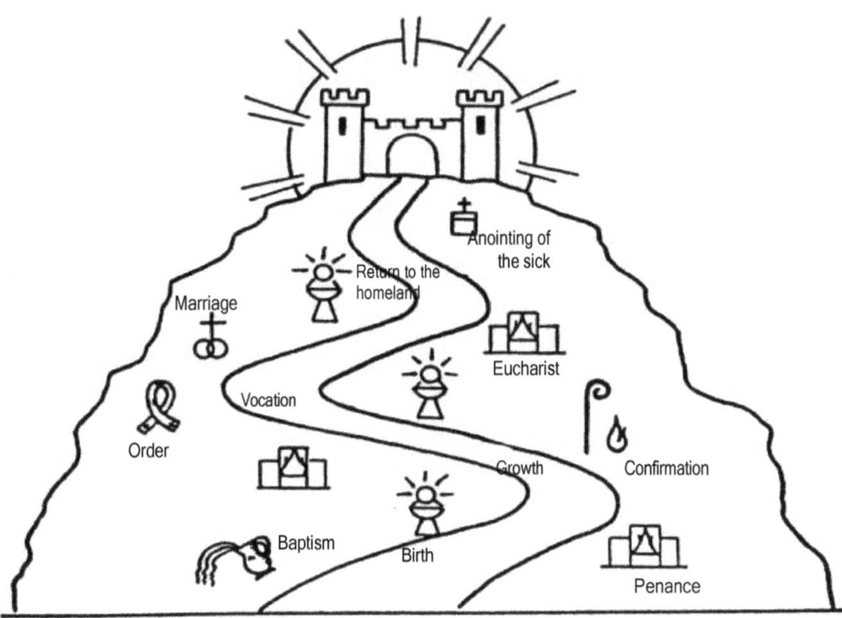

Through the sacraments, Christ accompanies us throughout our life's journey.

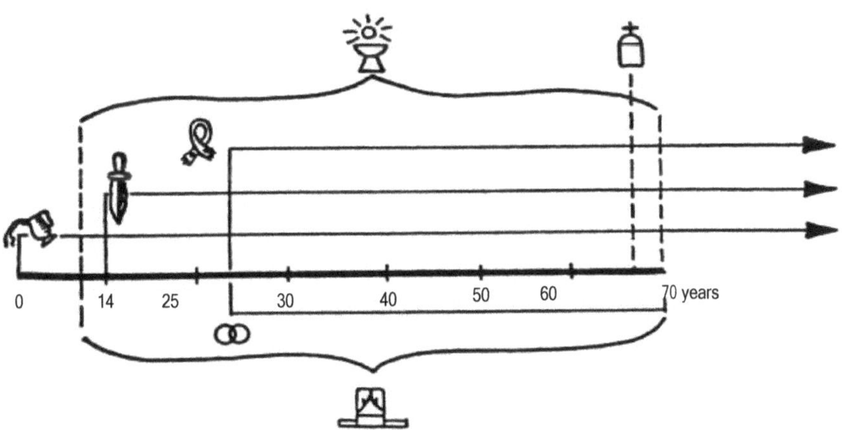

Note: This scheme shows us at what time of life each of the Sacraments comes to our aid. Baptism, Confirmation and Holy Orders imprint a character that remains even after death.

123.- What are the sacraments?
The sacraments are efficacious signs of grace instituted by Christ and entrusted to the Church to give us divine life and salvation.

124.- How many and which are the sacraments?
There are seven sacraments, and they are Baptism, Confirmation and Eucharist, Penance, and Anointing of the Sick; Holy Orders and Matrimony.

125.- How do the sacraments act as grace?
They act on their own, by the power that comes to them from Christ, independently of the one who administers them.

126-A.- What is sacramental character?
It is the spiritual seal that configures the recipient with Christ and is impressed by the sacraments of Baptism, Confirmation, and Holy Orders.

126-B.- What is a sacramental celebration?
It is a meeting of the Sons of God with their Father by means of rites already organized and established by the Church.

RECOMMENDATIONS

+ If you find an unobstructed path, it may lead you nowhere. (Vigil)

+ He who mocks and laughs at another, gains a small taste and a great enemy. (Quevedo)

+ He who undertakes nothing, concludes nothing. (Chaucer)

+ Science can be learned by heart, but wisdom cannot. (Sterne)

26. THE SACRAMENTAL CELEBRATION OF THE PASCUAL MYSTERY "We Christians celebrate the Victory of Christ, for it is our victory" (Lk. 22: 15-16)

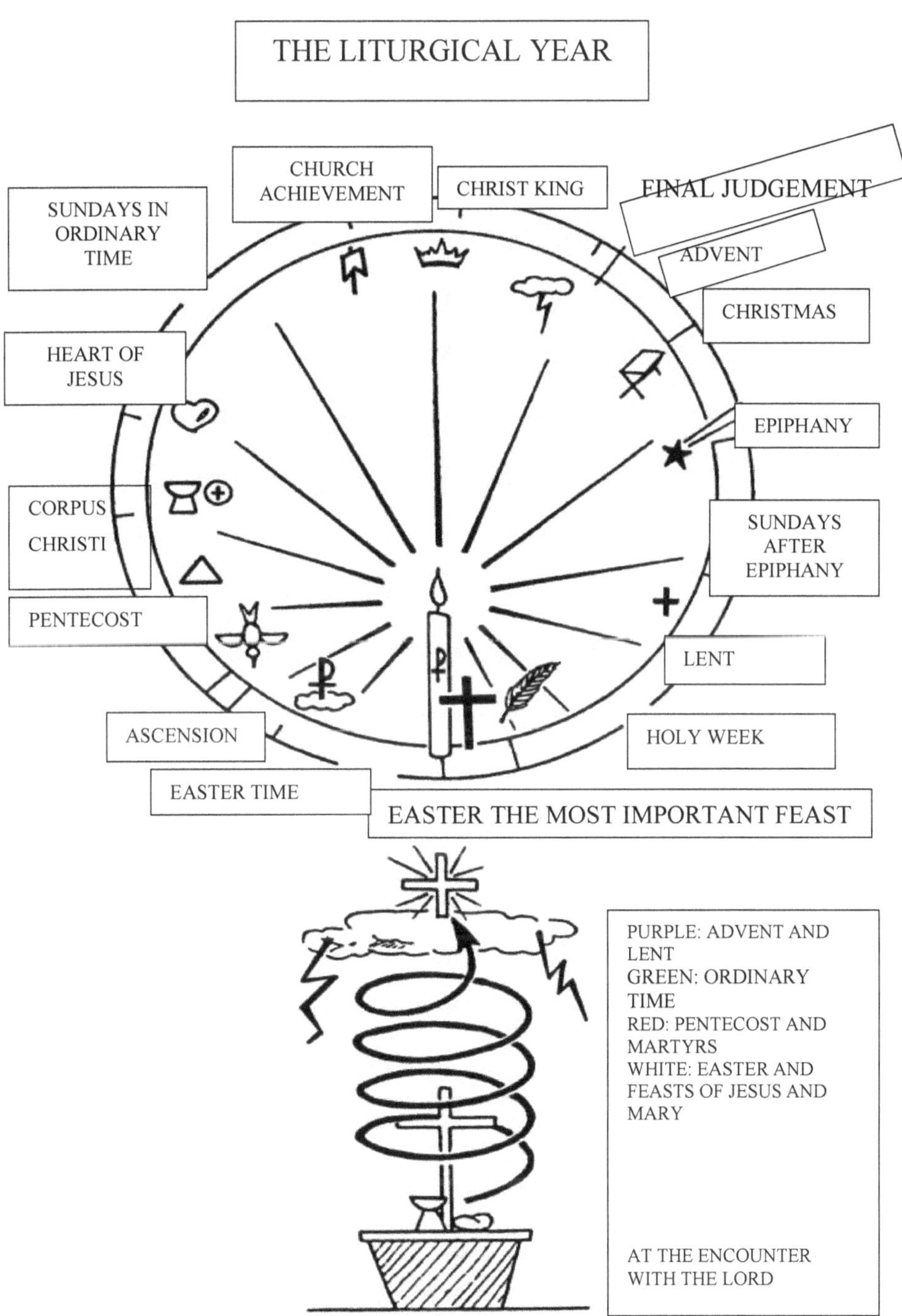

127.- How is this encounter expressed?
It is expressed through actions and words, for example the celebration of Holy Mass.

128.- Who celebrates the sacraments in the Church?
They are celebrated by the whole Church, that is, the Body of Christ, united to its Head, represented by the minister.

129.- What is celebrated in the liturgical year?
It celebrates the unfolding of the various aspects of the Paschal Mystery, accomplished by Christ and fulfilled in the saints.

130.- What is the Paschal Mystery?
It is the work of salvation accomplished by the life, death, and resurrection of Jesus Christ.
We must consider it as the most important feast of Christians because it gives meaning to all religious festivals.

131.- Why does the Church celebrate the feasts of the saints?
It celebrates them in order to unite with the Church in heaven, to glorify Christ in his saints, and to be stimulated by their example.

27. SACRAMENTS OF CHRISTIAN INITIATION: They guide us in the Church. "...receive more abundantly the treasures of the divine life and advance towards the perfection of charity." (Paul VI, Constitucion Divinae Consortium Naturae).

The Seven Sacraments

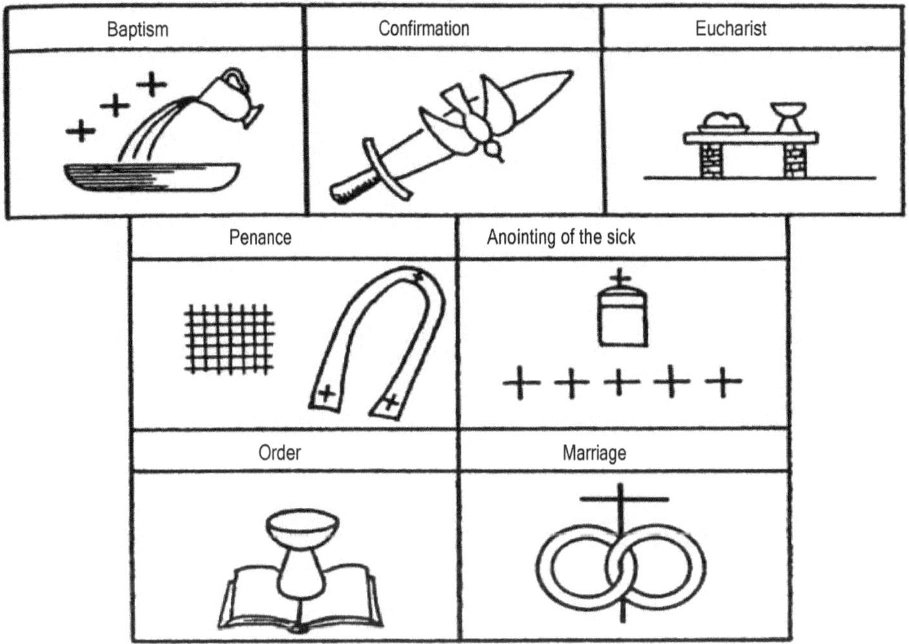

The three distinguishing marks of a Sacrament

1 External sign
   something seen and heard

2 Inner Grace
   the life of grace is given or increased

3 Institution by Jesus Christ a word of Christ

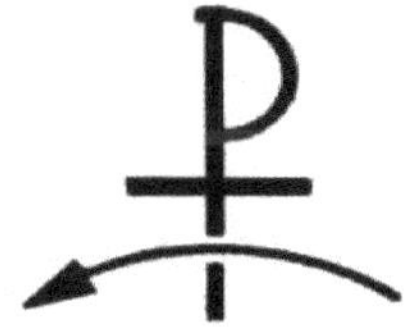

Only Christ alone can unite grace to an outward sign

132.- What are the sacraments of Christian initiation?
They are Baptism, Confirmation, and Eucharist. They are the beginning and foundation of the whole Christian life.

28. BAPTISM: "Thank you, Lord, for making me a Christian!"

BAPTISM

IS THE GATEWAY TO THE KINGDOM OF GOD

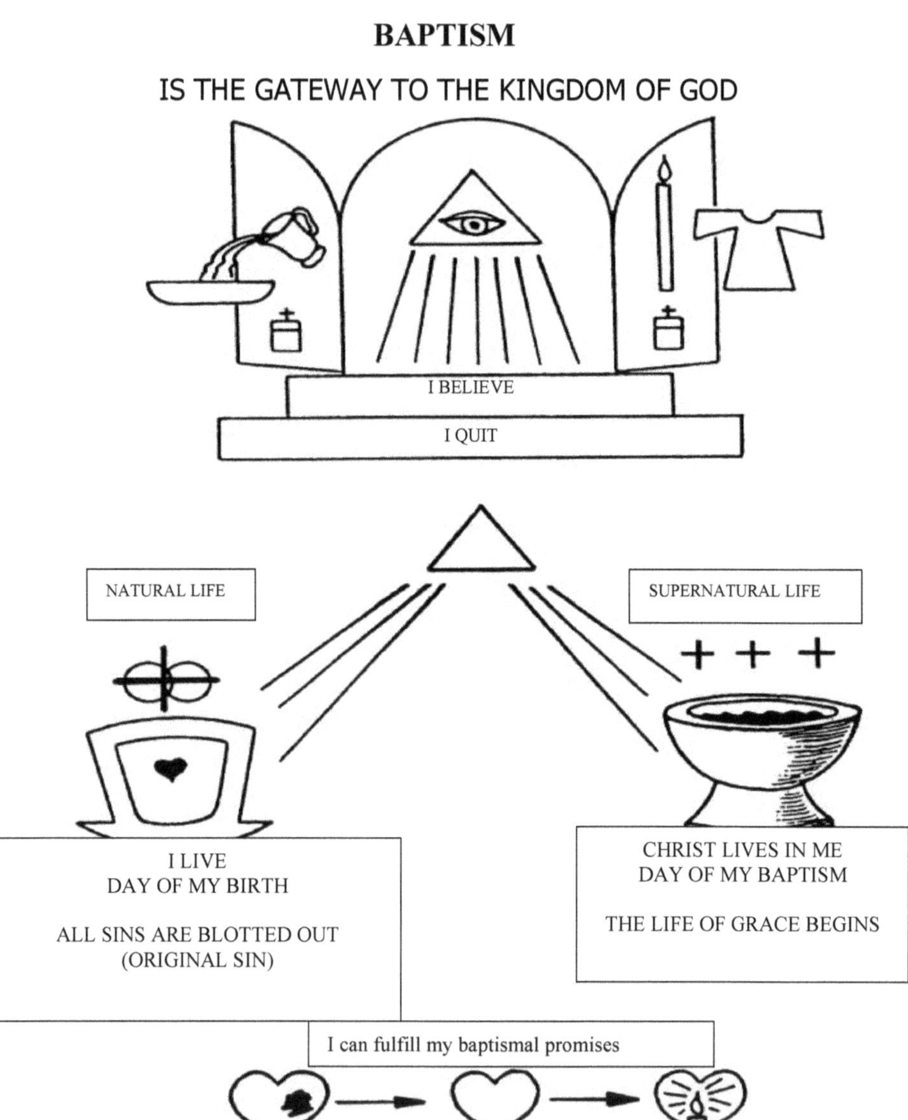

133.- What is baptism?

It is the sacrament of faith by which we are reborn to new life in Christ and made children of God.

134.- When did Christ institute baptism?

He instituted it when he said to the apostles: "Go therefore and make disciples of all nations, baptizing them in the name of the Father and of the Son and of the Holy Spirit" (Mt. 28:19-20).

135.- What are the fruits of baptism?

They are:

- The forgiveness of original sin and of any other sin, with the penalties due for them.
- It makes us children of God and heirs of heaven.
- Infuses sanctifying grace
- It imprints the sacramental character, and we are consecrated forever to God.
- We are incorporated into the Church.

136.- What does the rite of baptism consist of?

By immersing the candidate in water or pouring water over his head, invoking the Father, the Son, and the Holy Spirit.

137.- Who can baptize?

Ordinarily, the priest and the deacon, in case of emergency, may baptize any person who intends to do what the Church does.

<u>**EMERGENCY BAPTISM:**</u> There are many cases in our communities where children die without baptism due to distance and family situations. That is why we recommend that in case of death, the catechists or the parents themselves baptize the child, pouring natural (clean) water on the head, saying at the same time: **"N.... (**child's name**), I baptize you in the name of the Father and of the Son and of the Holy Spirit. Amen."**
It is not necessary for the child to have godparents or new clothes. All this will be done later if the child recovers and the priest is informed so that he can finish the other rites that were not done, and the baptismal certificate is entered in the parish baptismal book.

138.- Can anyone be saved without baptism?
Yes, those who sincerely seek God and strive to fulfill His will.

139.- When should infants be baptized?
As soon as possible, without being involved in economic or customary calculations. Parents are responsible for bringing their children to baptism as soon as possible.

140.- What are the requirements for taking a child to be baptized?
They are the following: 1º The parents must be married by the Church, 2º The godparents must be chosen among married or unmarried people, 3º A preparatory talk must be attended at least, 4º The child must be registered with the birth certificate or birth certificate and thus avoid mistakes.

141.- And those who have grown up without baptism, what should they do?
They should receive adequate preparation through lectures that are appropriate to their age and personal condition.

29.- CONFIRMATION: "Then they laid their hands on them and received the Holy Spirit" (Acts 8:17)

CONFIRMATION = STRENGTHENING

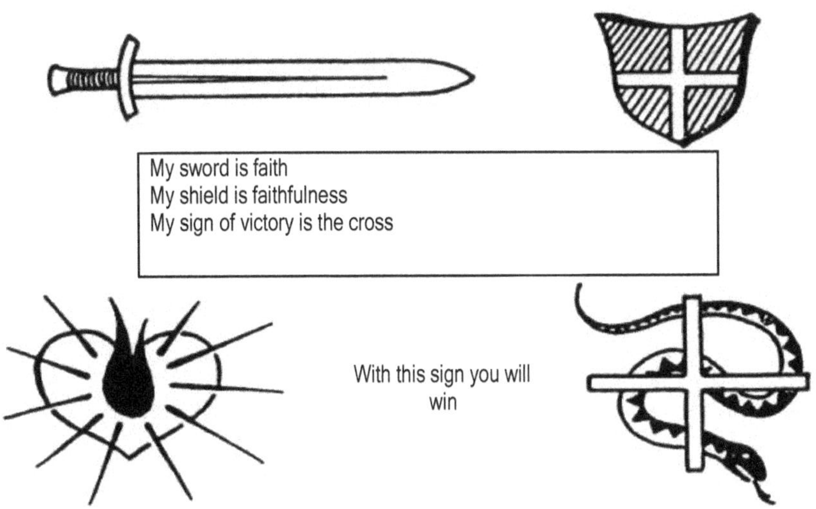

Confirmation is the sacrament by which a major decision is made

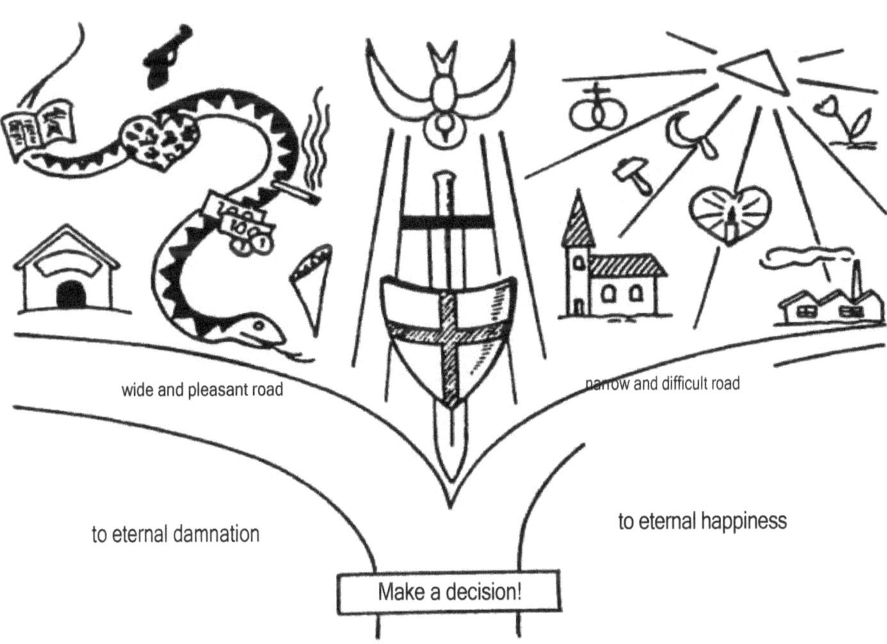

142.- What is confirmation?

It is the sacrament that perfects the baptismal grace by giving us the Holy Spirit, and we become soldiers of Christ.

143.- What are the effects of Confirmation?

The effects of Confirmation are to strengthen our divine filiation, to unite us more intimately to Christ and the Church, and to help us bear witness to our faith.

144.- Does confirmation imprint a character on the soul?

Yes, it imprints character, that is, the mark of the Holy Spirit to be a witness for Christ.

145.- What is the essential rite of confirmation?

It is the anointing with the holy chrism on the forehead of the baptized, with the imposition of the bishop's hand and the words: **"N.... (name), be sealed with the gift of the Holy Spirit".**

146.- What is required to receive confirmation?

It is required to profess the faith, be in a state of grace, be willing to receive the sacrament, be prepared to be a witness of Christ, and be at least 14 years old.

147.- Who can receive confirmation?

Every baptized person can and should receive confirmation.

148.- Who administers the confirmation?

It is ordinarily administered by the bishop or by a priest delegated by him and in case of danger of death, by any priest.

30. THE EUCHARIST: "Take and eat, this is my Body... take and drink, this is my blood... do this in remembrance of me" (permanent miracle) (1 Cor. 11: 23-26)

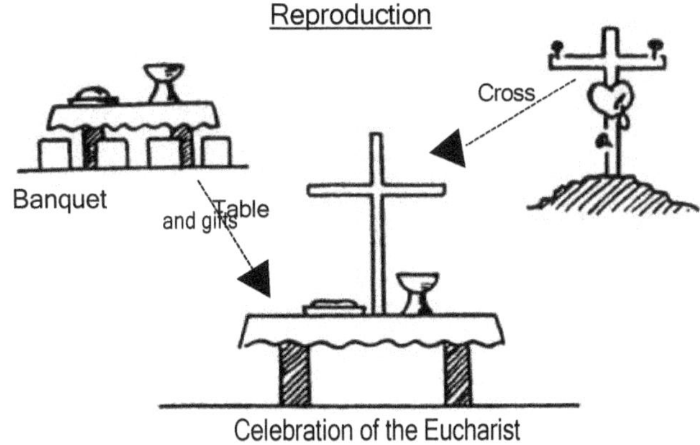

Sacrifice of the Cross - Sacrifice of the Mass

Sacrifice	Sacrifice of the Cross	Sacrifice of the Mass
offering	Christ	Christ
priest	Christ	Christ
place	Golgotha	Altar
mode	bloody	Bloodless
number	once	Countless times
character		

Glory to God and grace to us

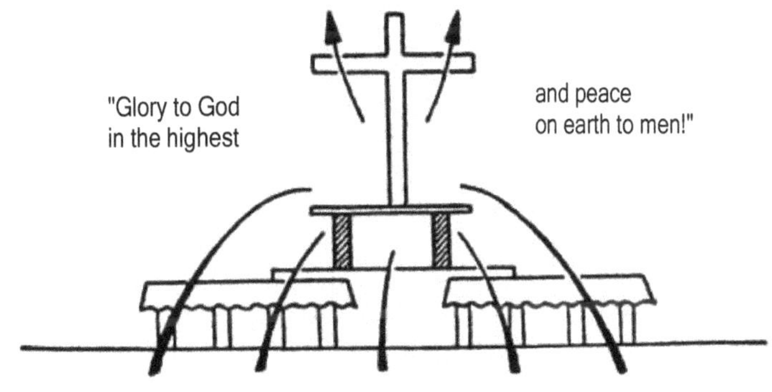

149.- When did Christ institute the Eucharist?
He instituted it at the Last Supper, on Holy Thursday.

150.- What is the Eucharist?
It is the sacrament of the Body and Blood of Christ under the species of bread and wine.

151.- What is contained in the Eucharist?
It contains Christ himself, alive and glorious, with his Body and Blood, his soul and divinity.

152.- What is the celebration of the Holy Mass?
It is the gathering of the Christian people in the Church to celebrate the paschal mystery: Christ's passion, death, and resurrection.

153.- What are the two parts of the Eucharistic celebration?
The two parts are the liturgy of the Word and the Eucharistic liturgy.

154.- What are the main elements of the liturgy of the Word?
These are the readings, the homily, and the universal prayer.

155.- What are the main elements of the Eucharistic liturgy?
They are the offertory, the consecration, and the communion.

156.- What is realized by consecration?
The transubstantiation of the bread and wine into the Body and Blood of Christ takes place. They become a sacred person, Jesus. This is a permanent miracle of God.

157.- Who can consecrate the Eucharist?
Only validly ordained priests, who serve as Christ among us.

158.- How is the sacrificial character of the Eucharist manifested?
It is manifested in the very words of the consecration pronounced by the priest: "THIS IS MY BODY WHICH WILL BE GIVEN UP FOR YOU," "THIS IS THE CHALICE OF MY BLOOD, THE BLOOD OF THE NEW AND

ETERNAL COVENANT, WHICH WILL BE POURED OUT FOR YOU AND FOR MANY FOR THE FORGIVENESS OF SINS."

159.- For what purposes is Holy Mass offered?
There are four purposes for which the Holy Mass is offered: to adore God, to thank him for his benefits, to ask him for gifts and graces, and to make satisfaction for our sins.

WORSHIP: God our Lord deserves all the praises and blessings from us because we are His children and we feel very happy to know that the Holy Mass is the most sublime act of worship that we can address to Him.
THANKSGIVING: It is well born to be grateful. The Holy Mass, called Eucharist, is a reason to give a thousand thanks to Jesus for staying with us and for the blessings with which He rewards us every day without deserving it. First of all, Life.
TO ASK HIM: We are limited and poor and we need his help, his mercy, that is why we have to trust fully in his power and humbly beg him for what is best for our happiness and salvation. He does listen to us.
SATISFY: "When a man bows his head before God, He crowns it" God is always a person and that is why the Lord's Supper is a reason to repent and convert our hearts.

STRUCTURE OF THE MASS

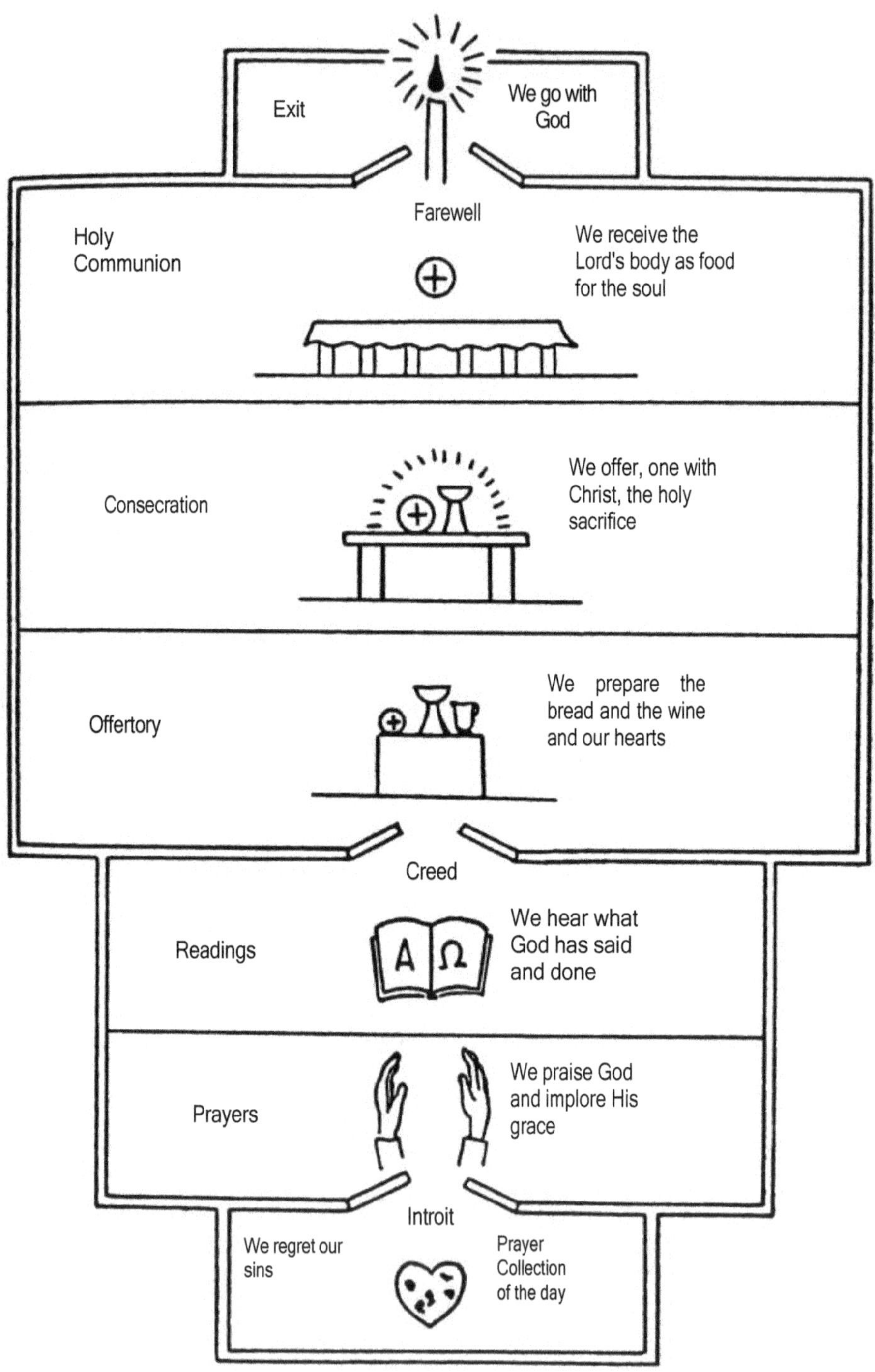

160.- What is sacramental communion?
It is to receive Christ himself who offers himself for us, under the species of bread and wine.

161.- What are the conditions for communion?
1st, To be in a state of grace without mortal sin. 2nd, to keep an hour of fasting by not eating anything one hour before communion, and 3rd, to know whom one is receiving.

162.- What are the effects of communion?
The effects of communion are to increase union with Christ and the Church, to forgive venial sins, and to preserve from mortal sins.

163.- Shall we visit Christ the Eucharist?
Yes, to manifest our gratitude, our love, and our adoration. Even if we live far away from the temple, we can visit Jesus spiritually by praying from wherever we are.

164.- When should children receive their First Communion?
Since they are of a reasonable and conscious age (nine or ten years old), they have received the appropriate preparation and are being confessed.

165.- To whom should the Viaticum be administered?
Viaticum is to be administered to the faithful who, for whatever reason, are in danger of death.

31. SACRAMENTS OF HEALING:
"God has mercy on all."

166.- What are the sacraments of healing, and what are they for?

They are penance and the anointing of the sick. They serve to continue in the Church the healing and saving work of Christ, the physician of our souls and bodies.

32. RECONCILIATION: "Whose sins you forgive, they are forgiven; whose sins you retain, they are retained" (Jn. 20: 22-23.)

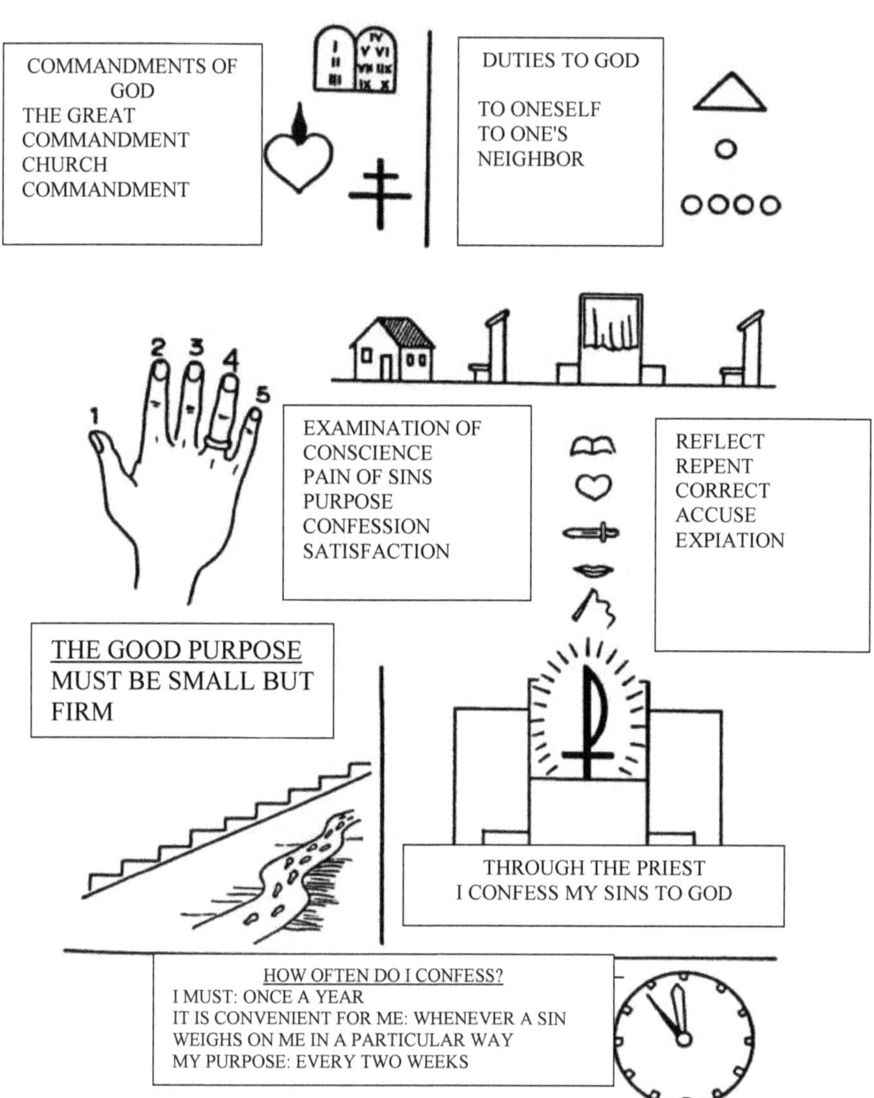

167.- What is the sacrament of penance?
It is the sacrament that grants forgiveness for sins committed after baptism, reconciling the sinner with God and the Church.

168.- Of what acts is the sacrament of penance composed?
It consists of five acts of the penitent:
1. Examination of conscience
2. Sorrow for sins
3. Proposal of amendment
4. Confession of sins
5. Fulfill penance

169.- What is the examination of conscience?
The examination of conscience is to remember the sins committed since the last well-done confession.

170.- What is the sorrow of sins?
The sorrow of sins is an inner feeling or sorrow of having offended God. It is called contrition.

171.- What is the purpose of amendment?
The purpose of the amendment is a firm resolution not to sin again and to avoid everything that could be an occasion for sin.

172.- What sins should be confessed?
All mortal sins must be confessed, with their number and circumstances. Venial sins should also be mentioned. If one forgets to confess a mortal sin, the confession is valid and must be said at the next confession, but whoever forgets to confess it out of shame commits a sacrilege (a very grave sin).

173.- What is satisfaction or penance?
These are the prayers or sacrifices that the confessor imposes on the penitent to repair the damage caused by the sin.

174.- What are indulgences?

They are the remission of temporal penalties for sins, which a Christian obtains for himself or for another through the mediation of the Church by means of works of charity, sacrifices, prayers, or certain devotions.

33. THE ANOINTING OF THE SICK: "Is anyone among you sick? Let him call for the priests of the church, that they may pray over him and anoint him with oil in the name of the Lord"

(Jas. 5:14)

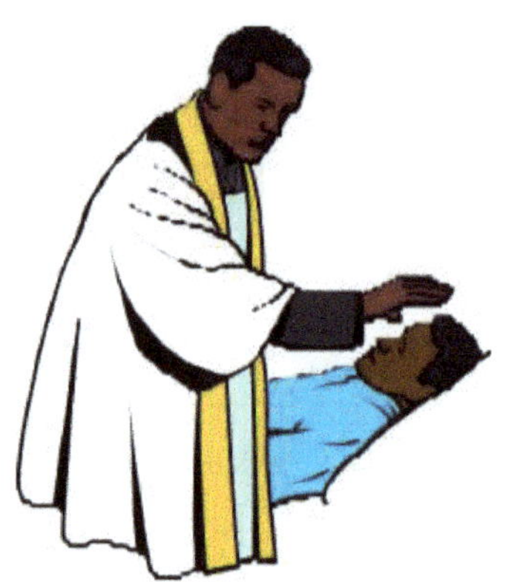

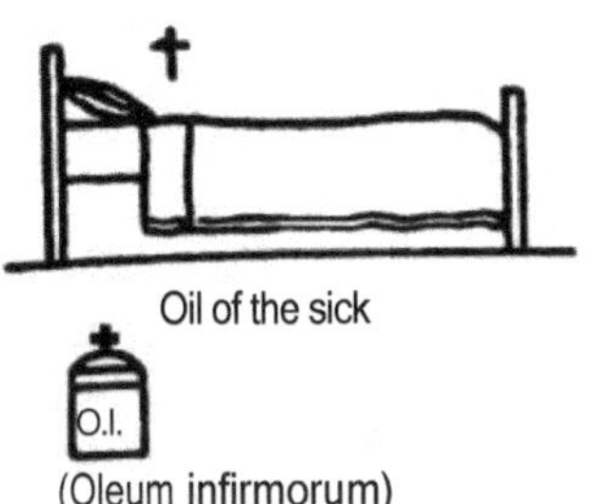

Oil of the sick

O.I.

(Oleum infirmorum)

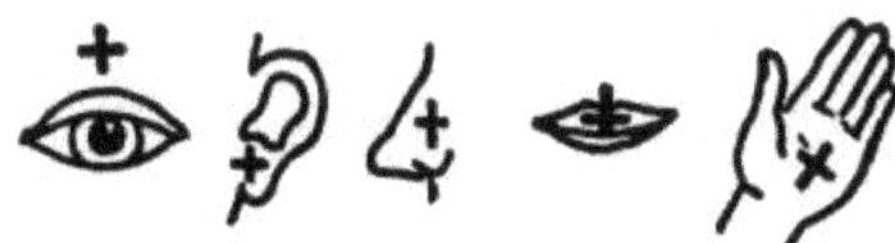

Today: Only on the forehead and palms

<u>Preparations for Holy Unction</u>

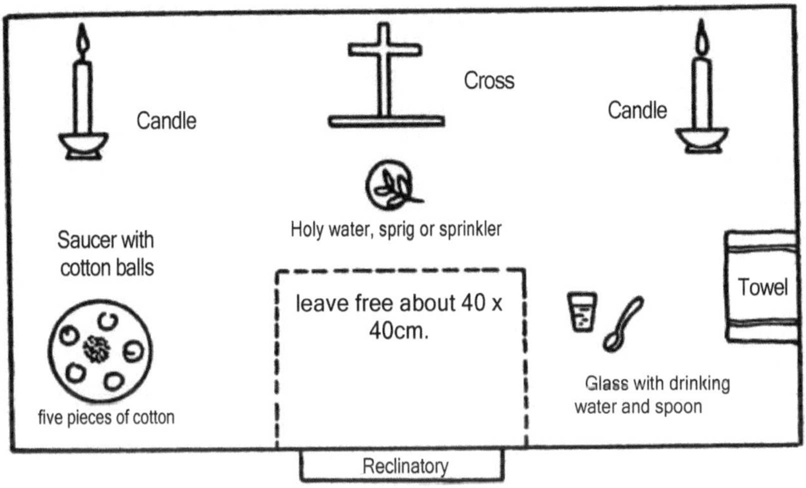

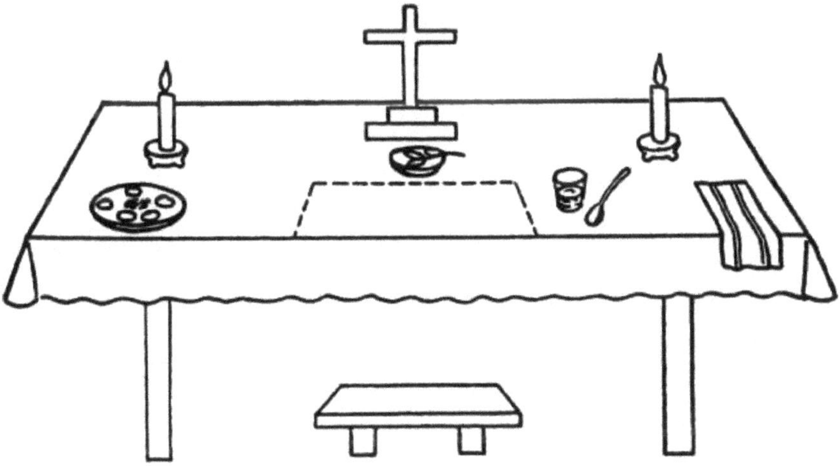

175.- What is the anointing of the sick?
It is the sacrament whose purpose is to confer a special grace on a Christian who is troubled by sickness or old age.

176.- When is the anointing of the sick to be received?
When the faithful begin to be in danger of death due to illness, accident, or old age. If he is going to undergo a delicate surgical operation, he may also receive the Anointing.

177.- Can the anointing of the sick be received several times?
It can be received when a Christian falls seriously ill and also when, after having received it, the illness worsens.

178.- What are the effects of the sacrament of the anointing of the sick?
The union of the sick person to the Passion of Christ; consolation and encouragement to endure sufferings in a Christian way; forgiveness of sins if he/she has not been able to go to confession; restoration of bodily health, if it is convenient for spiritual health and preparation for death.

179.- What should family members of a person in danger of death do?
They should be interested in seeking the health of his soul by calling a priest to attend to him spiritually and receive this great divine help.

34. OF COMMUNITY SERVICE: "To serve, serve"

180.- What are the sacraments at the service of the community?
These are the sacraments of Holy Orders and Marriage.

35. PRIESTLY ORDER: "Let us pray for the increase and holiness of priestly and religious vocations and for the fidelity of priests" (Acts 20: 28-30)

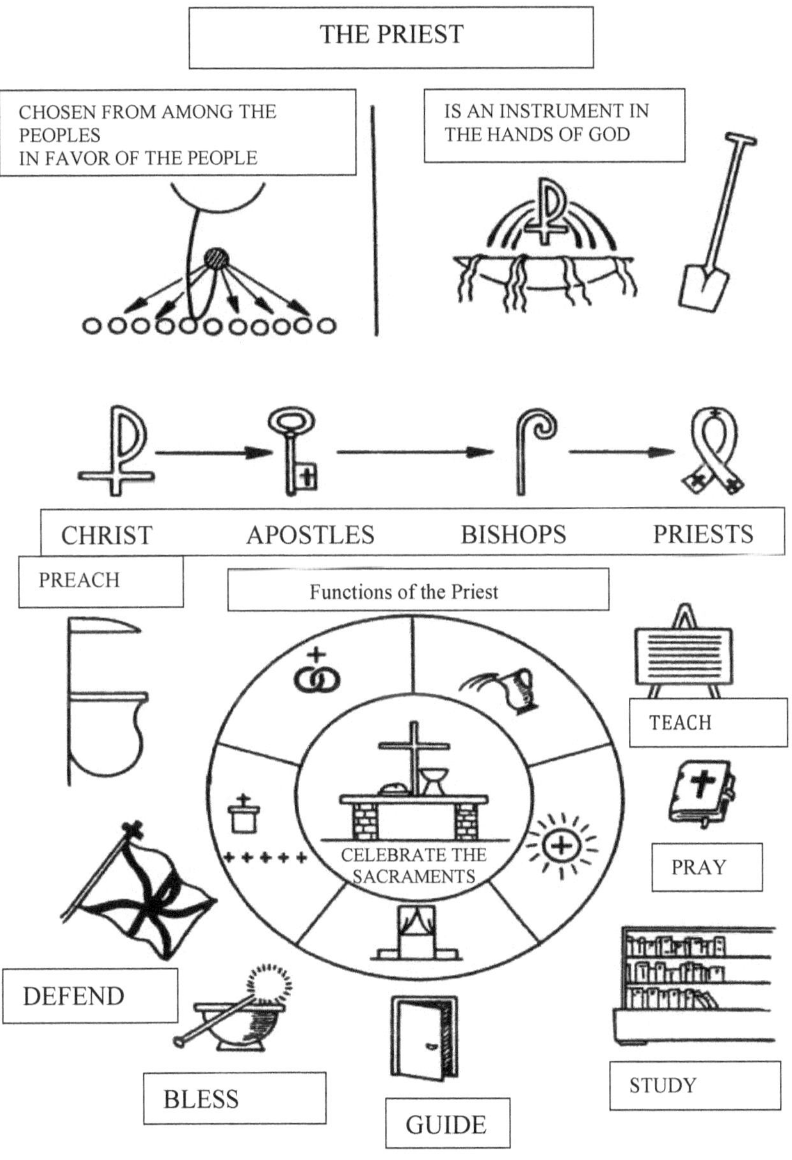

181.- What is order?
It is the sacrament that perpetuates the one priesthood of Christ until the end of time, by which some of the faithful are constituted sacred ministers.

182.- When did Jesus Christ institute the sacrament?
Jesus Christ instituted the sacrament of Holy Orders at the Last Supper with the words, "Do this in remembrance of me."

183.- Can one participate in the priesthood of Christ in various ways?
Yes, one can participate in two ways: the way common to all the faithful of the Church and called baptismal priesthood and the way proper to ordained ministers, which is divided into three degrees: that of Bishops, that of Priests, and that of Deacons.

184.- What is the proper task of the ministerial priesthood?
That of serving the Church and mankind in the representation of Christ the Head. They exercise it through teaching, the celebration of the Holy Mass, Confession, the administration of the other sacraments and by directing the faithful in what concerns God.

185.- Does the sacrament of Holy Orders imprint a character in the soul?
Yes, it imprints an indelible character.

186.- Who can receive the sacrament of Holy Orders?
Only baptized men, willing to freely embrace celibacy, whose aptitudes for the ministry have been duly recognized, can receive it. It is urgent that an abundance of priestly vocations arise from our districts and hamlets to serve God among the poorest and neediest.

36. MARRIAGE: "It is important that more value be placed on the need for marriage among Catholics"

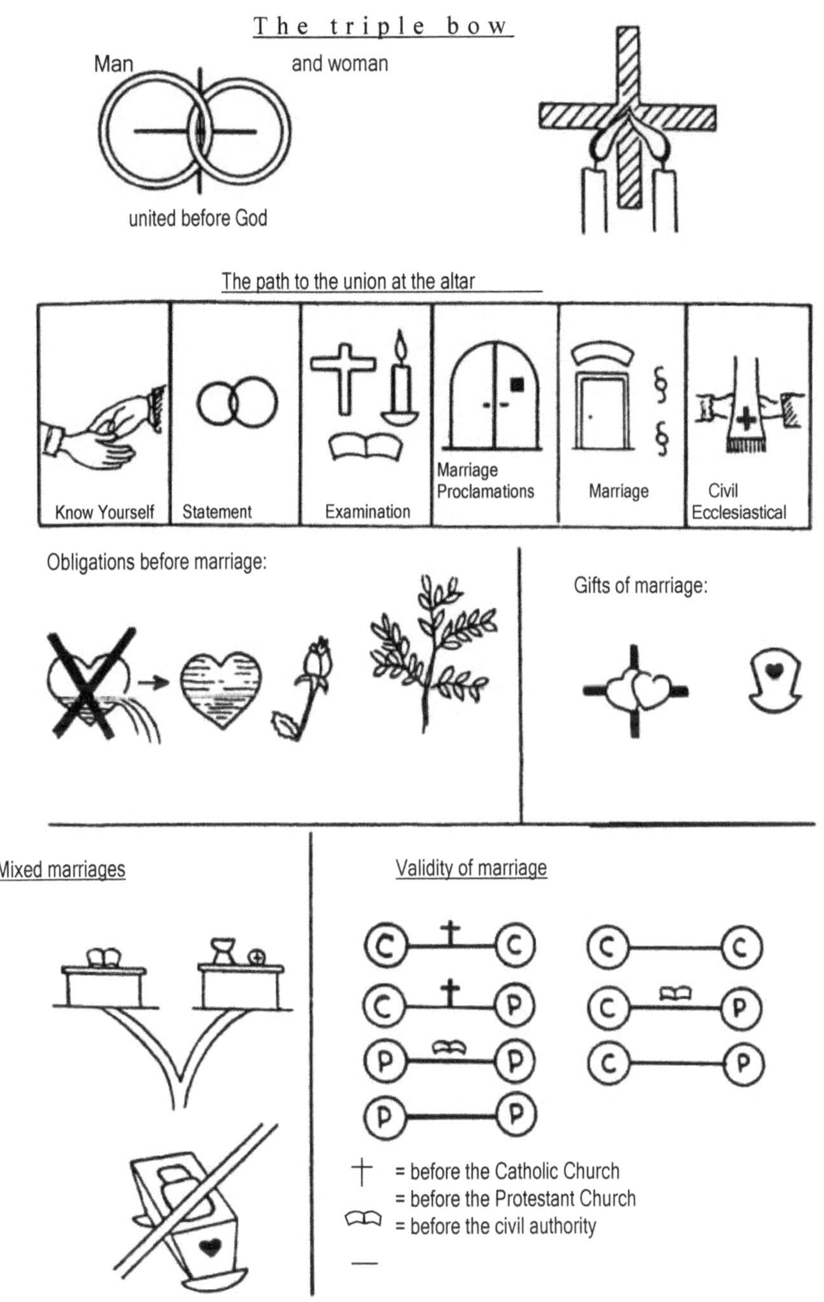

187.- What is marriage?
It is a sacrament by which God blesses the intimate community of life and love constituted by a man and a woman in the bosom of the Church. He grants them special graces to faithfully fulfill their duties as spouses and parents.

188.- What are the effects of the grace of the sacrament?
The grace of the sacrament perfects the human love of the spouses, reaffirms their indissoluble unity, and sanctifies them on the way to eternal life.

189.- Who administers the sacrament of marriage?
It is administered by the spouses themselves, expressing their mutual consent before the Church. The priest receives the consent of the spouses in the name of the Church and blesses the union.

190.- What does it mean that they are free to marry?
This means that they do not act under duress and are not impeded by natural or ecclesiastical law.

191.- Why does the Church require ecclesiastical marriage for the faithful?
Because marriage is a state of life in the Church, which creates rights and duties between spouses and towards their children, being Christians, they should be consistent with their faith and not let the idea of poverty or the current situation be greater than the love they have for each other, and they should formalize before God their situation.

192.- What is a marriage based on?
It is based on the will of the spouses to give themselves mutually and definitively to each other in order to live a faithful and fruitful covenant of love.

193.- What are the essential characteristics of marriage?
There are three:

1º **Unity** (Contrary to polygamy = having several women or men)

2º **Indissolubility** (Against divorce that breaks up families)

3º **Openness to fertility** (against the inhuman campaign of abortion and the artificial means of birth control that cause so much damage in our country)

194.- Why is the family called the "domestic church"?
It is so-called because the family is the place where children receive the first proclamation of the faith, and it is a school of human virtues and Christian charity. The healthy custom of praying the rosary, blessing food, and reading the Bible as a family should not be lost.

MARRIAGE REQUIREMENTS

1º Interview of the interested couple with a priest of the parish.
2º Presentation of documents: Baptismal certificate, copy of ID card.
3º Two witnesses who know the couple.
4º Participation in the role of Pre-marriage talks.
5º Confession of sins.

37. SACRAMENTALS:
"Let us promote these signs of sanctification of the Church"

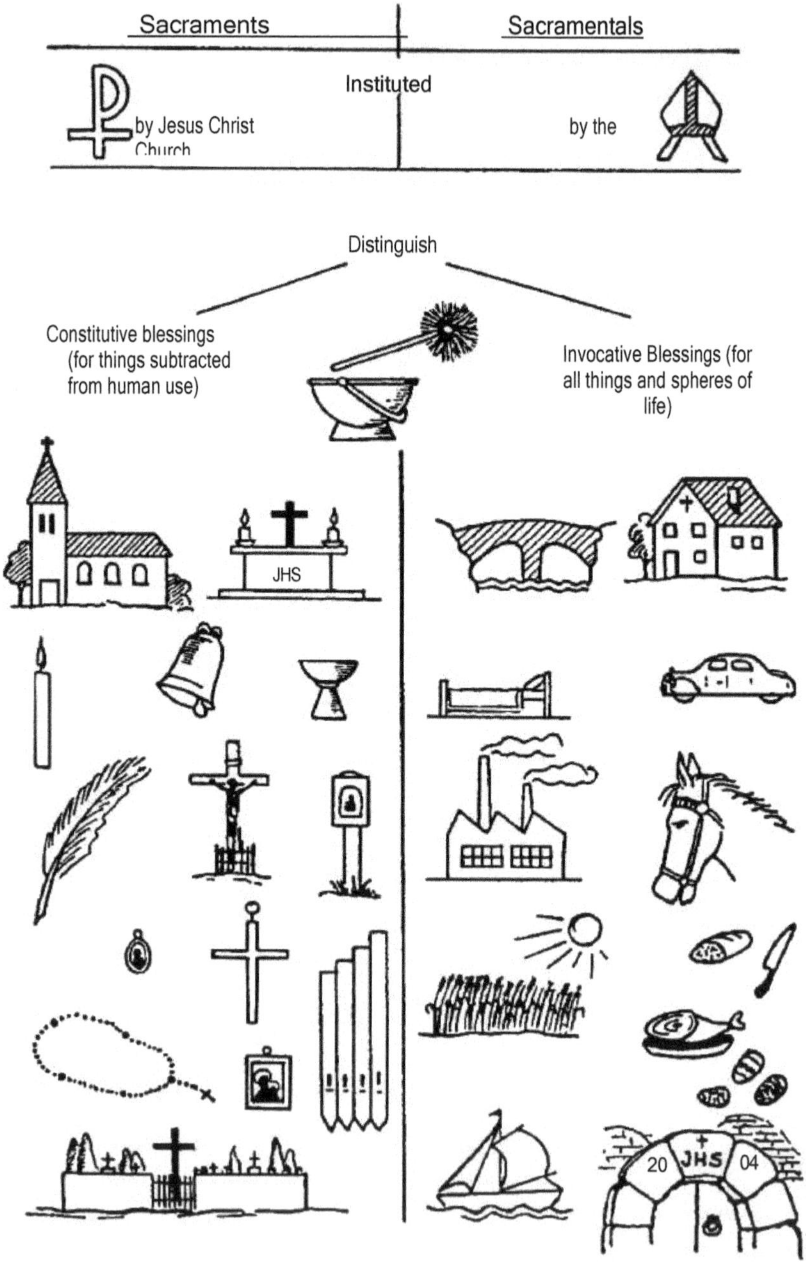

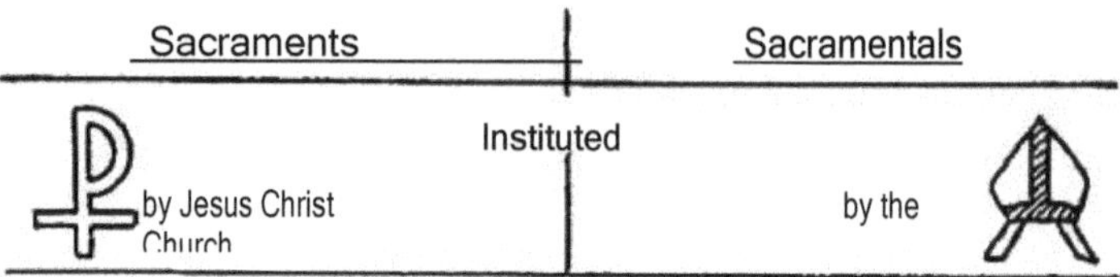

195.- What are sacramentals?

Sacramentals are sacred signs instituted by the Church. Their purpose is to prepare people to better receive the sacraments and to sanctify the various circumstances of life.

196.- What are the main sacramentals?

They are **blessings** (of people, animals, and objects) and **exorcism** (with which the presence of the demon in a person is rejected).

197.- Are there other forms of popular piety in the Church?

Yes, for example, the veneration of relics, pilgrimages, the Way of the Cross, the rosary, processions, scapulars, and medals.

PART THREE: LIFE IN CHRIST

CHAPTER I:
MAN'S VOCATION,
LIFE IN THE SPIRIT (Eph. 1: 4-5)

198.- What is man's vocation?
Man's vocation is to be happy forever with God.

38. THE DIGNITY OF THE HUMAN PERSON:
"In the image of God He created him" (Sir. 17: 3-7)

199.- On what is the dignity of the human person based?
The dignity of the human person is based on being created in the image and likeness of God and, therefore, on his vocation to holiness, which consists in following the voice of God that resounds in the conscience and impels him to do good and avoid evil.

200.- What is man created in the image of God for?
To attain eternal happiness, seeking its perfection in truth, goodness, and love.

201.- What is freedom?
Freedom is the power that God has given man to do deliberate acts on his own. Freedom in man is a sign of the divine image.

202.- Is there a right to exercise freedom?
Yes, every man enjoys this right, especially in moral and religious matters.

39. THE MORALITY OF HUMAN ACTS:
"My actions are personal" (Sir 17:11-14)

203.- What is a human act?
It is an act performed freely after a judgment of conscience. You have to think about what you are doing.

204.- How are these acts qualified?
They are morally qualified as good or bad.

205.- On what does the morality of human acts depend?
It depends on the object chosen, the end sought, and the circumstances of the action.
For the object chosen morally specifies the act of the will, according to reason recognizes it and judges it to be good or bad.

206.- What is the end or the intention?
It is that which is sought when acting.

207.- Does the end justify the means?
In no way, because an action does not cease to be bad because the end is good.

208.- What are the circumstances of a human act?
These are the elements that aggravate or diminish the goodness or malice of human acts.

209.- What does the morally good act cntail?
It assumes the goodness of the object, the end, and the circumstances.

40. MORAL AWARENESS:
"We all have a conscience" (Rom. 1:32)

210.- What is consciousness?

It is man's tabernacle, where he is alone with God, whose voice resounds in his innermost being. It commands her to do good and to avoid evil.

211.- What is the function of consciousness?
The function of conscience is to judge concrete choices, approving those that are good and denouncing those that are bad. It will always give us its judgment.

212.- Is it necessary to educate the conscience?
Yes, because the education of conscience guarantees freedom and engenders peace of heart because it formulates its judgments according to the true good willed by God the Creator.

213.- How is the conscience educated?
Conscience is educated by listening to the Word of God in prayer, examining our life in the light of the Gospel and with the help of a good counselor.

41. HUMAN VIRTUES:
"They must be obtained and lived with perseverance" (Phil. 4:8)

214.- What is virtue?
Virtue is a habitual and firm disposition to do good.

215.- What are human virtues?
The human virtues are stable dispositions of the human spirit, which regulate our acts, order our passions, and guide our conduct according to reason and faith. They are Prudence, Justice, Fortitude, and Temperance.

216.- What is prudence?
It is the virtue that disposes man to always discern the good and choose the good means to achieve it.

217.- What does justice consist of?
It consists of the constant and firm will to give to God and to one's neighbor what is due to them.

218.- What is strength?
It is the virtue that assures firmness and constancy in doing good in the face of difficulties.

219.- What is temperance?
It is the virtue that moderates the attraction to pleasure and the use of created goods.

220.- How do human virtues grow?
They grow through education and persevering effort under the action of divine grace. We can persevere by attending the sacraments and collaborating with the Holy Spirit.

42. THEOLOGICAL VIRTUES:

"Let us pray God to grant them to us" (1 Cor. 13:13)

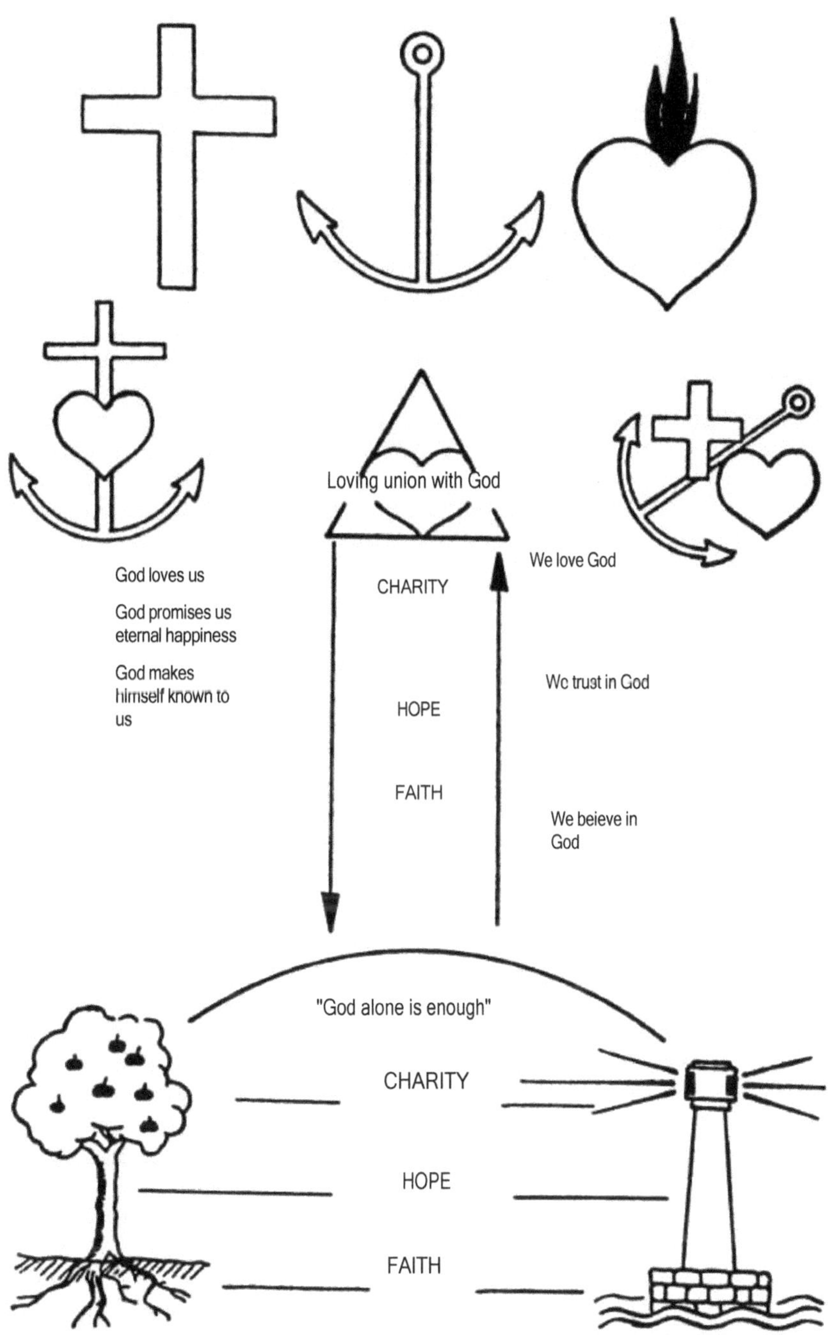

72

221.- What and what are the theological virtues?
These are the virtues that have God as their origin, motive, and object, and there are three of them: faith, hope, and charity.

222.- What is faith?
It is the theological virtue by which we believe in God and in all that He has revealed to us.

223.- What is hope?
It is the theological virtue by which we desire and expect from God eternal life and the graces to merit it.

224.- What is charity?
It is the theological virtue by which we love God above all things and our neighbor as ourselves for the love of God.

43. THE SIN:
"Let us not turn our backs on God our Father" (Jas. 1:13-15).

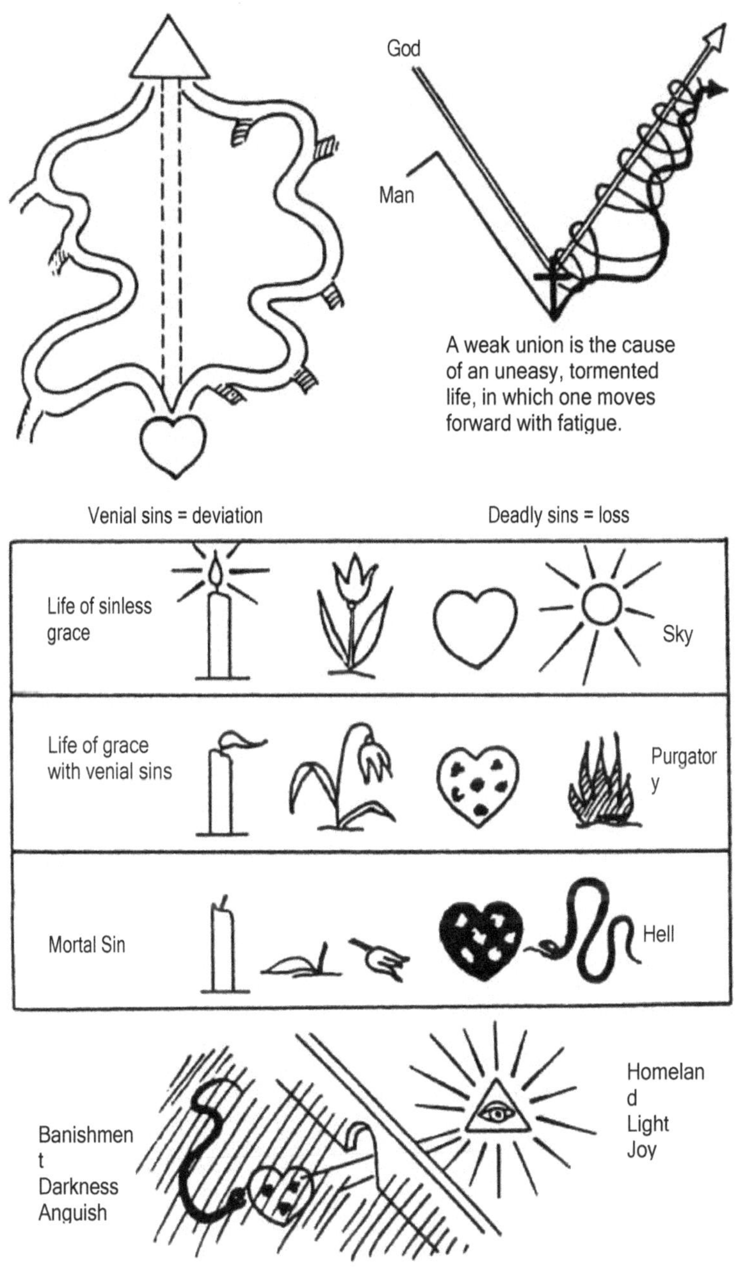

225.- What is sin?
Sin is an offense against the love of God, whom man disobeys, when he does evil with a word, thought, act, desire, or omission contrary to his law.

226.- According to their gravity, how can we divide sins?
We can divide them into mortal sins and venial sins.

227.- What is a mortal sin?
It is that sin that destroys charity in the heart of man by doing something gravely contrary to the law of God.

228.- What is a venial sin?
It is that sin that wounds charity in the heart of man by doing something slightly contrary to the law of God.

229.- What are the three conditions for a sin to be mortal?
A sin is mortal. When the matter is serious, there is full knowledge and free consent.

230.- What are the main vices? They are the seven deadly sins, namely pride and greed, envy, anger and lust, gluttony and sloth.

44. THE COMMUNITY AROUND US:
"Let us work for the common good of our land" (2 Tim. 4:1-2)

231.- Is man, the image of God, a solitary or a social being?
It is a social being called to form a human community. To grow and develop according to human nature.

232.- Is the human community the image of God?
Yes, there is a similarity between the union of divine persons and the union of men with each other.

233.- What is the principle, subject, and end of any society?
The principle, subject, and end of every society is and must be the human person.

234.- What is the task of a true partnership?
The task of an authentic society is to encourage the exercise of virtues and to respect the just hierarchy of values.

235.- What is the common good?
The set of conditions of social life that allow men to achieve more fully and easily their own perfection. The essential elements of the common good are three: 1st: respect for the rights of the person, 2nd: social welfare and development, and 3rd: peace and security.

236.- Are there differences between people?
They do exist, and they obey God's plan to foster charity toward one another. We should all respect others in their tastes and ideas.

237.- What is the principle of solidarity?
It is a requirement of the human and Christian fraternity, in favor of the most needy, sharing with them our spiritual and material goods.

45. THE MORAL LAW: "...the end of the law is Christ for the justification of every believer" (Rom. 10:4)

238.- What is the moral law?
It is a paternal instruction from God that indicates to man the ways that lead to beatitude and forbids the ways that lead away from God.

239.- Who is the fullness of the moral law?
The fullness of the moral law is Jesus Christ, the end of the law and the way to perfection.

240.- What is natural law?

It is a participation of the wisdom and goodness of God engraved in the soul of all men.

241.- What is the revealed law?

It is the law that God has given us in Sacred Scripture, and it comprises the Old Law and the New Law.

242.- What is the Old Law?

It is the first stage of revealed law, and its prescriptions are summarized in the Ten Commandments.

243.- What is the New or evangelical Law?

It is the grace of the Holy Spirit received through faith in Christ and contained in the commandment of love, thus fulfilling, surpassing, and bringing to perfection the Old Law.

YOU WILL NEVER REGRET IT

1	Do not speak ill of anyone.
2	Reflect well before deciding an issue.
3	Keep quiet when you feel angry.
4	Do not refuse a service that can be done.
5	To help those in need.
6	Confess your mistakes.
7	Be patient with everyone.
8	Do not fester in arguments.
9	Distrust what gossipers say.
10	Learn to call white what is white, black what is black, bad what is bad, and good what is good.
11	Learn to call sin sin and do not call it liberation progress, even if all fashions and propaganda would have you believe the opposite. (JOHN PAUL II)

46.- GRACE AND JUSTIFICATION: Let us allow the Holy Spirit to transform us with his graces and gifts (Rom. 7:22)

NEED FOR GRACE

Just as a light bulb needs electric current in order to illuminate...

Just as a plant needs sunlight in order to grow...

Just as each of the body's limbs needs blood from the heart in order to live...

Thus every man, in order to live as a child of God, must possess the GRACE of God

244.- What is justification?

It is the passage from sin to grace through the Passion, Death, and Resurrection of Jesus Christ. It comprises two aspects: first, conversion to God, and second, turning away from sin.

245.- What is grace?

It is a participation in the life of God and a help that God gives us to respond to our Christian vocation.

246.- How many kinds of grace are there?

There are two kinds of grace: habitual or sanctifying grace and actual grace.

247.- What is habitual or sanctifying grace?

It is a stable disposition that makes the soul capable of living with God and working for his love.

248.- What is actual grace?

It is an aid that God gives us to move us to conversion or to help us in the work of our sanctification.

249.- What are charisms?

They are special graces that are ordered to sanctify grace and to the common good of the Church.

250.- What is meant by merit?

It is the just retribution due for good work. But man by himself has no merit, but man's merit before God in the Christian life comes from the fact that God has freely disposed to associate man with the work of his grace.

CHAPTER II:
THE TEN COMMANDMENTS OF
GOD'S LAW

(Ex. 34:28; Dt. 4:13)

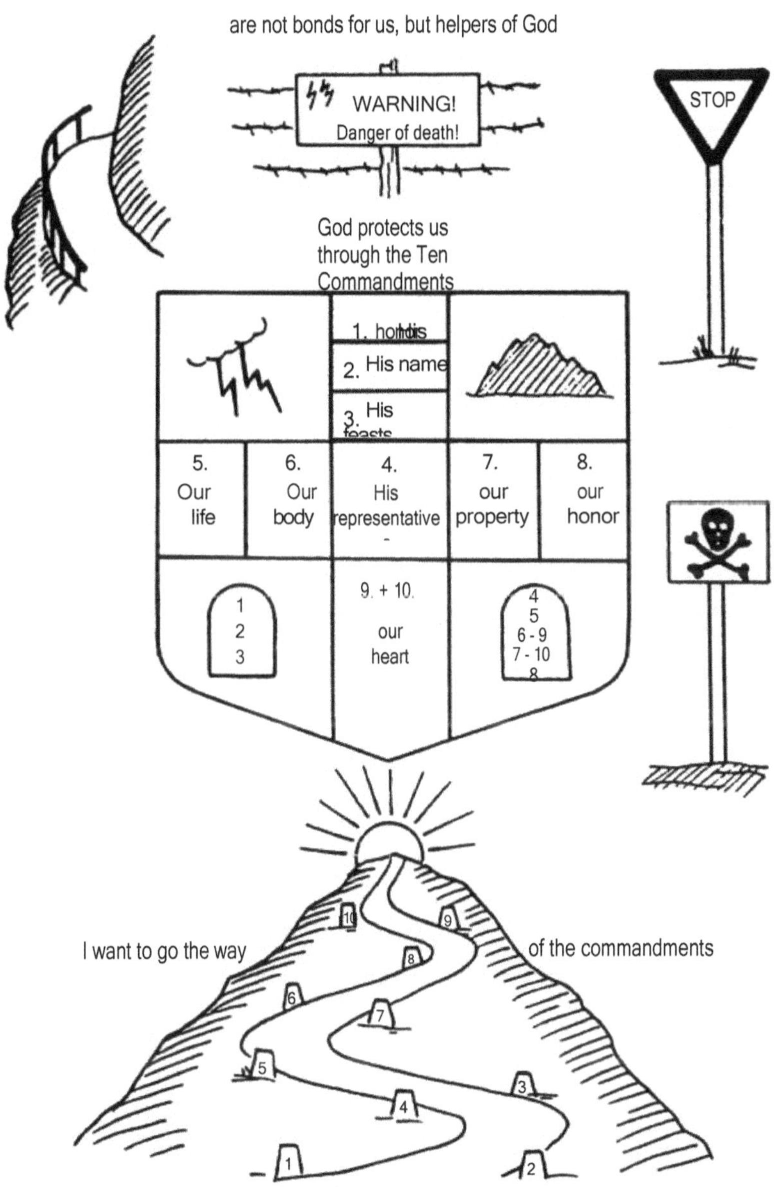

251.- What are the Commandments of God's law?
They are a gift from God in which the demands of the new covenant instituted by Christ are summarized and proclaimed.

252.- Do we have an obligation to keep the Commandments?
Yes, for Jesus himself declares, "If you would enter into eternal life, keep the commandments."

253.- What are the commandments of God's law?
The commandments of God's law are ten:
1. You shall love God above all things.
2. Thou shall not take God's name in vain.
3. Thou shall hallow the feasts.
4. Thou shall honor thy father and thy mother.
5. Thou shall not kill.
6. Thou shall not commit impure acts.
7. Thou shall not steal.
8. Thou shall not bear false witness or lie.
9. Thou shall not indulge in impure thoughts and desires.
10. Thou shall not covet the goods of others.

In short: "You shall love God above all things and your neighbor as yourself".

THOSE REFERRING TO GOD: "YOU SHALL LOVE THE LORD YOUR GOD WITH ALL YOUR HEART, WITH ALL YOUR SOUL, AND WITH ALL YOUR STRENGTH" (Mt. 22: 37).

47. 1ST COMMANDMENT:
" You shall love God above all things" (Ex. 20:3).

THOSE REFERRING TO GOD...

Strange Gods

in the past:

Currently

Superstition: Beware of witches and fortune tellers!

254.- What does the First Commandment command us?
It commands us to believe, trust, and love God above all things.

255.- What are the main sins against the first commandment?
The main sins are superstition, idolatry, divination, magic, sacrilege, simony, agnosticism, atheism, unbelief, heresy, and apostasy.

256.- What are the main sins against trust in God?
The main sins against trust in God are despair and presumption.

257.- What is a vow?
It is the free promise made to God about a good to be fulfilled. It is an act of devotion by which the Christian consecrates himself to God by promising a good deed.

258.- What is sacrilege?
It is to profane or treat unworthily the sacraments and other liturgical actions, as well as persons and places consecrated to God, especially the Eucharist.

259.- Is the worship of sacred images against the first commandment?
No, for the worship of images goes back to the persons who are represented in them and through them to God himself, the author of all holiness.

48. 2nd COMMANDMENT: "Thou shalt not take the name of God in vain" (Ex. 20:7)

260.- What does the Second Commandment command us?
It commands us to respect the name of God and all sacred things.

261.- What does the second commandment prohibit us from doing?
It forbids us the inconvenient use of the name of God and of Jesus Christ, of the Virgin Mary, and of all the saints, for example, blasphemy and bad words.

262.- What does the Second Commandment require us to respect?
It requires us to respect promises in the name of God and oaths that are legitimate.

263.- Who swears the name of God in vain?
He who swears falsely, taking God as a witness of what he affirms, and he who, after having promised something under oath, does not fulfill it.

264- What does it mean to swear falsely?
It means to make an oath without intending to keep it or, once made, not to keep it.

49. 3rd COMMANDMENT: "Thou shalt hallow the feasts" (Ex. 20:8)

Christian Customs

265.- What does the third commandment command us?
It commands us to dedicate Sunday and feast days to rest and to consecrate them to the service of God, especially to the Holy Mass.

266.- What is the meaning of these festivities?
The meaning of these feasts is to remember God's creative work, his salvific action in favor of mankind, and to oppose the servitude of work and the worship of money.

267.- What does the holy day of obligation mean?
It means that we are obliged to participate in the Mass unless we are impeded for just reasons.

268.- <u>For example:</u> What are the days of precept in Peru?
          January 1: St. Mary, Mother of God.
          June 29: St. Peter and St. Paul.
          August 30: Saint Rose of Lima.
          November 1st: All Saints Day.
          December 8: The Immaculate Conception.
          December 24: Christmas.

**THOSE THAT REFER TO THE NEIGHBOR:
YOU SHALL LOVE YOUR NEIGHBOR AS YOURSELF**

**50. 4th COMMANDMENT: "Honor thy father and thy mother"
(Ex. 20:12).**

"Am I my brother's keeper?"

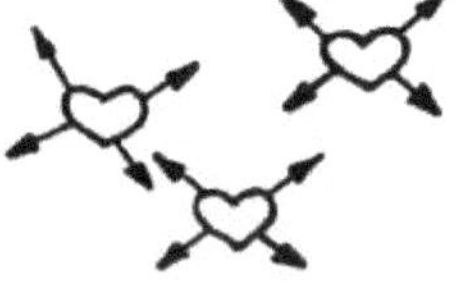

"Help each other carry
each other's burdens"

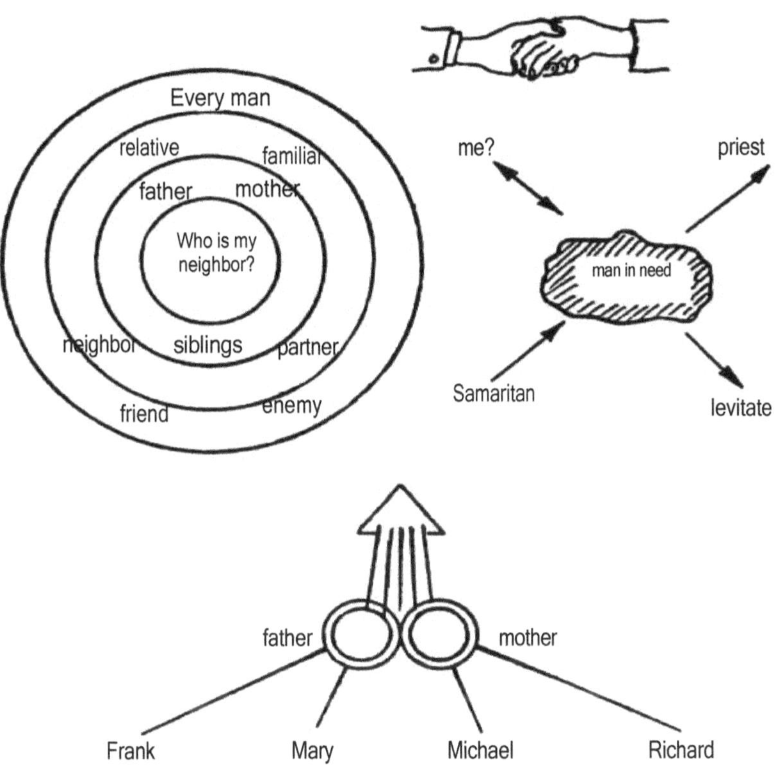

269.- What does the fourth commandment command us?
It commands us to honor and respect our parents and those whom God invests with authority for our good, for it is to them that we owe our Christian life and education.

270.- What are the duties of children to their parents?
Children owe their parents respect, gratitude, just obedience, and material and moral help in old age and sickness.

271.- What are the duties of parents towards their children?
Parents should educate their children in the faith, in prayer, and in virtues and attend, as much as possible, to their material and spiritual needs.

272.- What are the duties of civil authorities towards citizens?
To respect the rights of the human person, to administer justice with respect for the rights of each person, and to govern according to the requirements of the common good.

51. 5th COMMANDMENT: "Thou shalt not kill" (Ex. 20:13).

273.- Why can't a man kill another man?
Because human life is sacred, for it is created in the image and likeness of God.

274.- Since when is human life sacred?
From conception to death.

275.- What are the sins against the fifth commandment?
The sins against the fifth commandment are voluntary manslaughter, abortion, euthanasia, and suicide. It also forbids scandal, drug use, terrorism and torture, war, and the arms race.

276.- What does the fifth commandment ask of Christians?
The fifth commandment asks of Christians: respect for one's own life and the life of others, care for one's own health, respect for the dead, and the defense of peace.

THE CRIME OF ABORTION

Today, millions of innocent human beings are killed before birth and cold-bloodedly expelled from the womb simply because they were not wanted or because the child is seen as a burden to the family. This fact is the worst murder man has ever invented, and God condemns this in the Bible: On the slaughter of the innocent: Proverbs 6: 16-17: "The Lord utterly abhors the hands that shed innocent blood." Genesis 9:6: "Whoso sheddeth man's blood, by man shall his blood be shed: for in the image of God was man made."

52. 6th COMMANDMENT: "Thou shalt not commit impure acts" (Ex. 20:14).

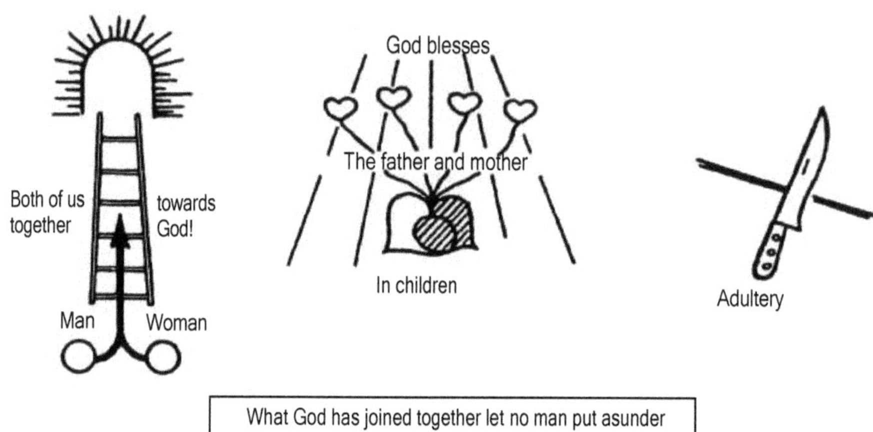

What God has joined together let no man put asunder

CHASTITY =

Mastery of the sexual instinct

MODESTY =

Protection of chastity

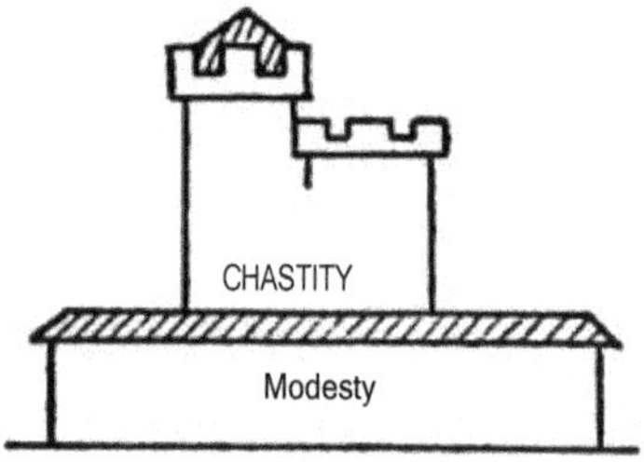

277.- What does the Church understand by the sixth commandment?
The Church understands the whole of human sexuality, regulated by virtue of chastity.

278.- What is chastity?
It is a moral virtue and a gift from God, by which the human being integrates sexuality in the person and avoids any behavior that may harm it.

279.- Should all Christians be chaste?
Yes, we must all be chaste, each according to his state in life.

280.- What are the main offenses against chastity?
They are the following: lust and masturbation, fornication, and pornography, prostitution, rape, and homosexual practices.

281.- What is human sexuality ordered to?
It is ordered to the conjugal love of man and woman within marriage.

53. 7th COMMANDMENT: "Thou shalt not steal" (Ex. 20:15).

282.- What does the seventh commandment command?
It commands the practice of justice and charity in the use of earthly goods and of the goods created by man. It also commands respect for all creation: animals, plants, and minerals, which God has placed in the world to help and serve man.

283.- What does the seventh commandment prohibit?
The seventh commandment prohibits theft, cattle rustling, bribery, breach of contract, paying an unfair wage, forgery of checks and invoices, wastefulness, willful damage to public property, and any act that leads to the enslavement of other human beings.

54. 8th COMMANDMENT: "Thou shalt not bear false witness nor lie". (Ex. 20:16).

284.- What does it send us?
Always tell the truth to others.

285.- What is the truth?

It is the virtue of being truthful in deeds and words, avoiding duplicity and hypocrisy.

286.- What are the sins against the eighth commandment?
The sins against the eighth commandment are false witness and rash judgment, libel and slander, boasting or vainglory, flattery, lying, and manipulation.

287.- What does the lie consist of?
It consists of saying something false with the intention of deceiving those who have the right to the truth.

55. 9th COMMANDMENT: "Thou shalt not consent to impure thoughts and desires" (Mt. 5:8).

288.- What does the ninth commandment ask of us?
He asks us for purity of heart to see all things according to God.

289.- How does the Christian consider his body and the body of others?
As a temple of the Holy Spirit and a manifestation of divine beauty.

290.- By what means must the Christian struggle to be pure of heart and overcome the concupiscence of the flesh? With prayer, with chastity (modesty), and with purity of gaze and intention.

291.- What is modesty?
It is the virtue by which the intimacy of the person is preserved, protecting the mystery of his love and ordering the looks, gestures, and words.

56. 10th COMMANDMENT: "Thou shalt not covet another's goods". (Ex. 20:17).

292.- What does the tenth commandment prohibit?
It forbids the covetousness of the good of others and the inordinate desire for wealth and power.

293.- And what does it command?
It commands us to practice benevolence, humility, and trust in God, banishing from the heart any form of envy.

294.- How can we overcome our disordered attachment to the goods of this world?
By being poor of heart and quenching our thirst for happiness in God.

57. THE PRECEPTS OF THE CHURCH:
They help us to fulfill God's law

295.- What are the main precepts of the Church?
The principal precepts of the Church are five:
1º To hear Mass in its entirety on all Sundays and holy days.
2º To confess mortal sins at least once a year when one is to receive Communion and in danger of death.
3º To receive Communion once a year, preferably at Easter time.
4º To fast and abstain from eating meat when commanded by Holy Mother Church.
5º To contribute to the support of the Church to the extent of one's possibilities.

PART FOUR:
PRAYER IN THE CHRISTIAN LIFE

CHAPTER I: PRAYER IN THE CHRISTIAN LIFE

(Job. 8:5; Ps. 119 y 147)

296.- What is prayer?

Prayer is the elevation of the soul towards God. It consists simply in speaking to God, either mentally or with the lips, and telling Him what we feel in our hearts at any time and place. A Christian should pray every day.

58. THE UNIVERSAL CALL TO PRAYER:
A necessity (1 Cor. 13:1-3).

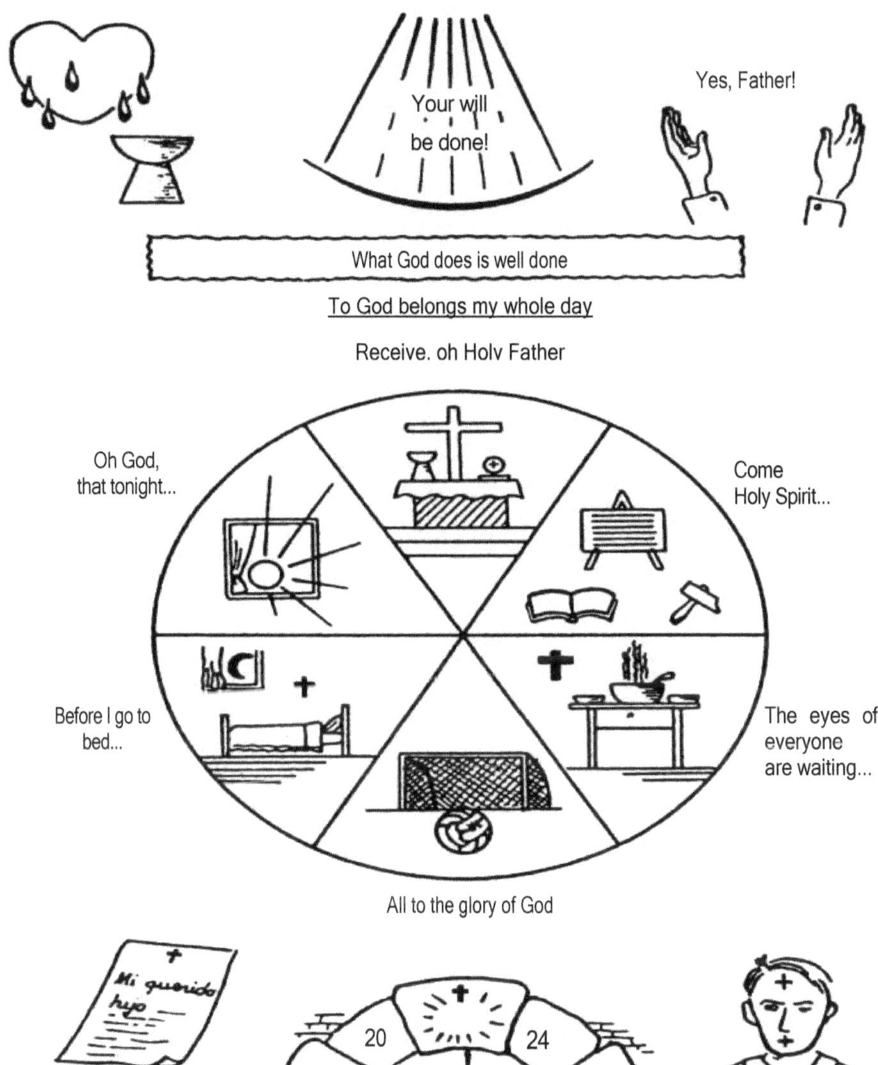

297.- When should we pray?
We should always talk to God, especially when we get up when we rest, when we go to lunch, when we leave the house, the Angelus at noon when we visit the Blessed Sacrament, the Holy Rosary, meditation... as well as some personal devotion.

298.- What is the perfect model of prayer in the New Testament?
The perfect model is the prayer of Jesus to the Father. It teaches us to pray with faith, and filial audacity, with humility and constancy, seeking only to do God's will.

299.- What are the forms of prayer with which the Holy Spirit instructs His Church?
There are five, namely, blessing, petition, intercession, thanksgiving, and praise.

300.- What is the prayer of blessing?
The one in which man blesses God, the source of all blessing.

301.- What about the petition?
It is that prayer that has as its object forgiveness, the coming of the Kingdom, or any true need.

302.- What does intercessory prayer consist of?
It consists of a request on behalf of another, whoever he or she may be.

303.- What does the prayer of thanksgiving consist of?
It consists in thanking God for every joy and every sorrow, every event and every need.

304.- What is the prayer of praise?
It is the prayer in which we glorify God, not only for what He has done but for what He is.

59. PRAYER LIFE:
It is our daily bread (Jn. 17).

305.- What are the most common expressions of Christian prayer?
There are three: vocal prayer, meditation, and contemplation.

306.- What is vocal prayer?
It is the prayer that is made by means of words but with the heart set on the One to whom we speak.

307.- What is meditation?
It is that prayer that seeks with thought and imagination, with emotion and desire, to appropriate and live the why and how of the Christian life.

308.- What is contemplation?
Contemplation is the gaze of faith, fixed on Jesus, whose word is listened to in silent and active love, in union with the prayer of Jesus Christ.

309.- When should we pray?
Always, because prayer is a vital necessity, inseparable from the Christian life.

60. THE LORD'S PRAYER:
"Lord's Prayer" (Mt. 6: 9-13).

310.- What is the fundamental prayer of the Christian?
It is the "Our Father" taught to us by Jesus Christ, a teacher and model of prayer.

311.- What does **Our Father** mean?
It means that this prayer puts us in communion with God the Father and reveals us as children of God and brothers and sisters in Christ.

312.- What does it mean "**that you are in heaven**"?
It does not signify a place but the majesty of God and his presence in the heart of all the righteous.

*** 3 Petitions that have as their object the glory of the Father:**

313.- What do we ask for when we say "**hallowed be thy Name**"?
We ask that God be recognized as holy by us and by all men.

314.- And when do we say "**Thy Kingdom come**"?
We ask for the growth of the Kingdom of God in our lives, the return of Christ, and the final coming of his Kingdom.

315.- What do we ask for when we say "**Thy will be done**"?
We ask her to unite our will to that of her Son, to carry out his plan of salvation in the world.

* 4 Petitions presenting our desires to the Father:

316.- What do we ask for when we say: "**Give us this day our daily bread**"?
We ask for the earthly food necessary for all and also for the Bread of Life, that is, the Word of God and the Body of Christ.

317.- What are we asking for when we say: "**Forgive us our trespasses**"?
We ask God's forgiveness, which he will give us if we, too know how to forgive, following the example and with the help of Jesus Christ.

318.- What are we asking for when we say: "**Lead us not into temptation**"?
We ask God not to let us take the path that leads to sin and to grant us the grace of final perseverance.

319.- What do we ask for when we say: "**Deliver us from evil**"?
We ask God to manifest his victory over the devil and to deliver us from all past, present, and future evil.

320.- What do we express when we say: "**Amen**"?
We express the wish that the seven petitions be fulfilled.

DEVOTIONAL

Prayer is a pleasant, loving, and trusting dialogue with the one we know loves and understands us.

THE LIFE OF A CHRISTIAN

WE ARE ALL CALLED TO HOLINESS:
"Be perfect as your heavenly Father is perfect" (Mt. 5:48)

"All the faithful, whatever their state or regime of life, are called to the fullness of the Christian life and to the perfection of charity" (CCC 2013). If we want to correspond to the universal call to holiness, we must strive to be pious, with a concrete plan of prayers and devotions that will lead us to have a contemplative life, especially taking advantage of the nature of our countryside.

To sanctify ourselves in our daily lives, we need to grow in the spiritual life, especially through prayer, mortification, and work.

(1) THE CATHOLIC MAN IS A MAN OF PRAYER:
"It is good to pray at all times and not to lose heart." (Lk. 18:1)

If God is life for us, it should not surprise us that our existence as Christians must be interwoven with prayer. But let us not think that prayer is an act that is fulfilled and then abandoned.

"The just man finds his pleasure in the law of Yahweh and tends to conform himself to that law day and night. In the morning, I think of You, and in the evening my prayer is directed to You like incense. The whole day can be a time of prayer: from evening to morning and from morning to evening. Even more: as Holy Scripture reminds us, even sleep must be prayer".

"The life of prayer must also be based on a few moments a day, dedicated exclusively to dealing with God in the midst of our ordinary daily life as simple people" (Christ Is Passing By, 119).

(2) LIFE OF SACRIFICE:

"If any man will come after me, let him deny himself, and take up his cross, and follow me." (Mt. 16:24)

The way of perfection passes through the Cross. There is no holiness without renunciation and spiritual combat. Spiritual progress involves struggle and mortification, which gradually lead to living in the peace and joy of the beatitudes (CCC 2015).

<u>**(3) WORK LIFE:**</u>
Man is created to work (Gen. 1:28; Wis. 9:1-3)

Human work proceeds directly from persons created in the image of God and called to prolong, unite, and for mutual benefit, the work of creation, dominating the earth. Work is, therefore, a duty: "If anyone is unwilling to work, let him not eat either." Work honors the Creator's gifts and the talents received. It can also be redemptive. By bearing the burden of work, in union with Jesus, the carpenter of Nazareth, and the crucified one of Calvary, man collaborates in a certain way with the Son of God in his redemptive work. He shows himself to be Christ's disciple by carrying the Cross every day in the activity he is called to perform. Work is a means of sanctification and of animating earthly realities in the spirit of Christ (CCC: 2427).

(4) THE LIFE PLAN OF EVERY CATHOLIC

The first thing we have to do to be good Christians is to try to live in the grace of God, avoiding all mortal sin, and since we want to love God above all things, we will even try to avoid all venial sin. A plan of **Christian life** lived with seriousness and interest can be the means to ensure that our life is neither useless nor sterile so that we live as true children of God.

<u>**Therefore, take into account the following so that you can apply it to your Christian life:**</u>

<u>**Each day**</u>:

• Have a fixed bedtime and wake-up time.
• Offer to God the day under the intercession of the Virgin Mary.
• A time of mental prayer (10 minutes). Preferably in the morning.
• Attend Holy Mass and receive Communion whenever possible.
• At noon, pray the *Angelus* (during the Easter Season the *Regina Coeli*).
• Pray the Holy Rosary, if possible, as a family.
• Read for a few minutes, at leisure, the New Testament or a spiritual book.
• Before going to bed, examine briefly how the day went. Pray three Hail Marys.
• To sanctify ordinary work, doing it well for the glory of God.

<u>**Each week:**</u>

- Sunday is the Lord's Day. Holy Mass should be the center of the day. It is also a day dedicated especially to the family, to rest, and to one's own spiritual enrichment.
- If it is not possible to attend Mass, participate in the Liturgy of the Word in our Chapel together with other faithful.
- It is highly advisable to receive Communion on Sundays and holy days of obligation.

<u>**Each month:**</u>

- To confess, with true repentance, even if there are no mortal sins, in order to receive sacramental grace. Do not forget that in the Promises, one always confesses.
- Receive spiritual direction from a learned, prudent, and experienced priest or an older, right-living person.
- Day of spiritual retreat: to dedicate a few hours to consider our relationship with God. In the presence of the Blessed Sacrament, if possible, or contemplating nature and reading the Holy Bible.

<u>**Each year:**</u>

- Retreat course or spiritual exercises: two or three days in silence, conversing alone with God, to achieve a new conversion. The soul, like the body, needs to regain strength.
- Attend the formation course for every Catholic organized by the Parish.
- At least an approach to the parish which allows us to work in coordination with our ecclesiastical jurisdiction.

<u>**At all times:**</u>

- Maintain the presence of God with ejaculatory prayers, spiritual communions, and acts of love and reparation.
- To consider that we are God's children: to try to please him in everything we do, as a child tries to please his father.
- Thank God for all that He gives us.
- To do everything for the love of God: to purify our intention with acts of contrition and atonement for our own and others' sins.
- To behave as we would like to have behaved at the hour of death. Then, we will not be afraid of death, and we will die as we have lived.
- Constant study of the Word of God and of the topics of our formation courses.

(5) SPECIAL DEVOTIONS FOR EACH DAY OF THE WEEK

Sunday: The Holy Trinity:
Attend Holy Mass fervently and receive Communion if possible.

Monday: **The Souls in Purgatory:** Pray for the souls of your relatives, friends, and benefactors.

Tuesday: **The Guardian Angels:** Go often to the Guardian Angels, asking them for help. Pray to your Guardian Angel.

Wednesday: **St. Joseph:** Invokes St. Joseph as the patron saint of the good death.

Thursday: **The Most Holy Eucharist:** Throughout the day, make frequent spiritual communions and, if possible, a visit to the Blessed Sacrament.

Friday: **The Passion and Death of Jesus Christ:** Meditate on the Passion and Death of the Lord using, for example, the Stations of the Cross. Perform some mortifications to unite yourself to the pain of Christ, such as not eating meat.

Saturday: **The Blessed Virgin Mary:** Pray the Salve or other Marian devotion.

THE HOLY MASS

Priestly Ornaments

Preparation of the Altar

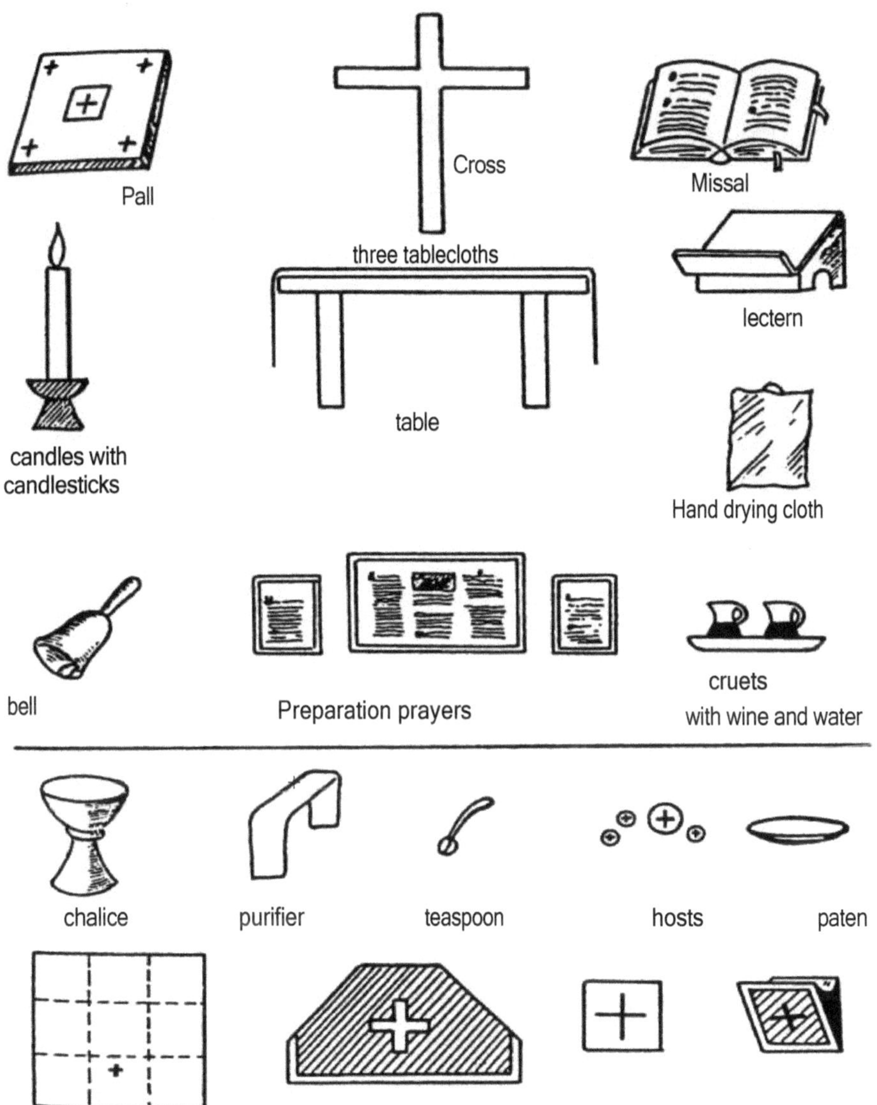

THE LITURGICAL LIFE OF EVERY CATHOLIC:

(6) THE HOLY MASS

The Mass is the renewal of the death of Jesus on the cross for our Salvation. God wants to nourish us with His Word (Readings) and with His Body (Communion) to give us his life and strength so that we may live our Catholic faith sincerely. We are all obliged to participate in Holy Mass on Sundays, Holy Days of Obligation, and in the Promises of the Sacred Heart of Jesus (Apostleship of Prayer). Those who are unable to do so because of distance should at least participate in the Masses celebrated in their community for the Patronal Feast. Here are the most important steps of the celebration so that we can learn them and thus participate actively in each Eucharist. Let us not forget that singing is important in every celebration. We should be interested in learning many songs.

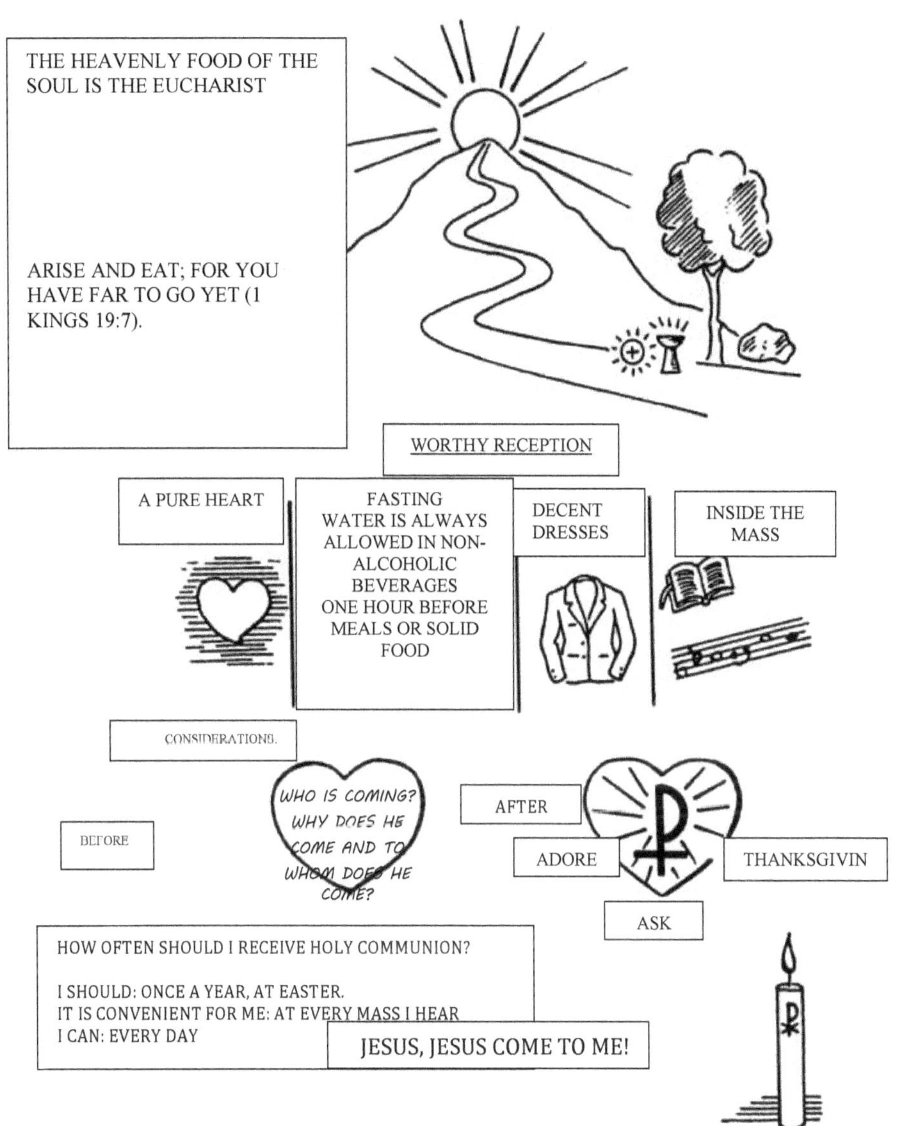

THE HEAVENLY FOOD OF THE SOUL IS THE EUCHARIST

ARISE AND EAT; FOR YOU HAVE FAR TO GO YET (1 KINGS 19:7).

HOW OFTEN SHOULD I RECEIVE HOLY COMMUNION?

I SHOULD: ONCE A YEAR, AT EASTER.
IT IS CONVENIENT FOR ME: AT EVERY MASS I HEAR
I CAN: EVERY DAY

JESUS, JESUS COME TO ME!

THE LORD'S DAY – THE MASS

* Entrance song...   Standing 

GREETING

<u>Priest:</u> **In the name of the Father +, and of the Son, and of the Holy Spirit.**

<u>People respond:</u> **Amen.**

P.- The grace of our Lord Jesus Christ, the love of the Father, and the communion of the Holy Spirit be with you all.

P.- And with your spirit.

PENITENTIAL ACT

P.- Bretheren, let us acknowledge our sins and so prepare ourselves to celebrate the sacred mysteries.

I confess before Almighty God and to you, my brothers and sisters, that I have greatly sinned, in my thoughts and in my words, and what I have done and what I have failed to do,

(Beating their breasts, they say:) **Through my fault, through my fault, through my grievous fault;**

(Then they continue:) **Therefore, I ask Blessed Mary ever-Virgin, all the angels and saints, and you, my brothers and sisters, to pray for me to the Lord our God.**

P.- May almighty God have mercy on us, forgive us our sins, and bring us to eternal life.

P. - Amen

LORD, HAVE MERCY

P. Lord, have mercy	P. Lord, have mercy
P. Christ, have mercy	P. Christ, have mercy
P. Lord, have mercy	P. Lord, have mercy

*** GLORIA** (On Sundays or important holidays, the hymn is sung or said:)

*** COLLECTED PRAYER** (At the end of the hymn, the priest, with joined hands, says:)

P.- **Let us pray** (The prayer of the day and ends:)

Through our Lord Jesus Christ, your Son, who lives and reigns with you in the unity of the Holy Spirit and is God forever and ever.

P.- **Amen**.

<u>LITURGY OF THE WORD</u>   Seated

*** FIRST READING**

- Reading of...
 At the end: **The word of the Lord.**
All: **Thanks be to God.**
*** RESPONSORIAL PSALM (First read the antiphon that will be repeated after each stanza, such as:** "Here I am, Lord, I come to do your will."
*** SECOND READING** (Read on certain feast days, solemnities, and Sundays)
- Reading of......
At the end, the reader says: **The word of the Lord.**
All acclaim: **Thanks be to God.**

ALLELUIA OR HYMN BEFORE THE GOSPEL   Standing

*** GOSPEL**
The minister: **The Lord be with you.**
The people respond: **And with your spirit.**
Reading of the Holy Gospel according to St. ....
The people shout: **Glory to you, O Lord.**

At the end: **The Gospel of the Lord.**
All shout: **Praise to You, Lord Jesus Christ**

* FAMILY   Seated

* PROFESSION OF FAITH   Standing

I believe in God, the Father almighty, Creator of heaven and earth. I believe in Jesus Christ, his only Son, our Lord, who was conceived by the power and grace of the Holy Spirit, was born of the Virgin Mary, suffered under Pontius Pilate, was crucified, died and was buried, descended into hell, on the third day rose again from the dead, ascended into heaven, and is seated at the right hand of God, the Father almighty. From there, he will come to judge the living and the dead. I believe in the Holy Spirit, the holy catholic Church, the communion of saints, the forgiveness of sins, the resurrection of the body, and the life everlasting. Amen.

* UNIVERSAL PRAYER

EUCHARISTIC LITURGY

* ALTAR PREPARATION AND OFFERINGS   Seated

P.- Blessed are you, O Lord, God of all creation, for through your goodness we have received the bread we offer you: fruit of the earth and work of human hands, it will become for us the bread of life.

P.- Blessed be God forever.

P.- Blessed are you, Lord God of all creation, for through your goodness we have received the wine we offer you: fruit of the vine and work of human hands, it will become our spiritual drink.

P.- Blessed be God forever.

P.- Pray, Bretheren, that my sacrifice and yours may be acceptable to God the Almighty Father.

P.- May the Lord accept this sacrifice at your hands for the praise and glory of his name, for our good and the good of all his holy Church.

* PRAYER OVER THE OFFERINGS   Standing

Then the priest, with outstretched hands, says the prayer over the offerings, always ending with the brief conclusion.

P.- Amen.

* EUCHARISTIC PRAYER

P.- The Lord be with you.
The people answer: **And with your spirit.**
The priest, raising his hands, continues: **Lift up your hearts.**
The people respond: **We lift them up to the Lord.**
He, with outstretched hands, adds: **Let us give thanks to the Lord our God.**
The people respond: **It is right and just.**
P.- It is truly right and just... (Continues the preface for each date)

* SAINT

Holy, Holy, Holy Lord God of Hosts. Heaven and earth are full of your glory. Hosanna in the highest. Blessed is he who comes in the name of the Lord. Hosanna in the highest.

EUCHARISTIC PRAYER III
(We have chosen this prayer because it is the most commonly used)

P.- You are indeed Holy, O Lord, and all you have created rightly gives you praise, for through your Son our Lord Jesus Christ, by the power and working of the Holy Spirit, you give life to all things and make them holy, and you never cease to gather a people to yourself, so that from the rising of the sun to its setting a pure sacrifice may be offered to your name.

(He places both hands on the bread and the chalice) **Kneeling**

Therefore, O Lord, we humbly implore you: by the same Spirit, graciously make holy these gifts we have brought to you for consecration, that they may become the Body and Blood of your Son our Lord Jesus Christ, at whose command we celebrate these mysteries.

(Takes the host and says)

For on the night he was betrayed, he himself took bread, and, giving you thanks, he said the blessing, broke the bread, and gave it to his disciples, saying:

TAKE THIS, ALL OF YOU, AND EAT OF IT, FOR THIS IS MY BODY, WHICH WILL BE GIVEN UP FOR YOU.

(Takes the chalice and says)

P-In a similar way, when supper was ended, he took the chalice, and giving you thanks, he said the blessing, and gave the chalice to his disciples, saying:

TAKE THIS, ALL OF YOU, AND DRINK FROM IT,
FOR THIS IS THE CHALICE OF MY BLOOD,
THE BLOOD OF THE NEW AND ETERNAL COVENANT WHICH WILL
BE POURED OUT FOR YOU AND FOR MANY FOR THE
FORGIVENESS OF SINS.

DO THIS IN MEMORY OF ME

P. The mystery of faith:

**We proclaim your Death, O Lord,
and profess your Resurrection
until you come again.**

Or:

**When we eat this Bread and drink this Cup, we proclaim your Death, O Lord,
until you come again.**

Or:

**Save us, Savior of the world,
for by your Cross and Resurrection you have set us free.**

Therefore, O Lord, as we celebrate the memorial of the Saving Passion of your Son, his wondrous Resurrection and Ascension into heaven, and as we look forward to his second coming, we offer you in thanksgiving this holy and living sacrifice.

Look, we pray, upon the oblation of your Church and, recognizing the sacrificial Victim by whose death you willed to reconcile us to yourself, grant that we, who are nourished by the Body and Blood of your Son and filled with his Holy Spirit, may become one body, one spirit in Christ.

May he make of us an eternal offering to you so that we may obtain an inheritance with your elect, especially with the most Blessed Virgin Mary, Mother of God, Mother of God, with your blessed Apostles and glorious Martyrs

(with Saint N: *the Saint of the day or Patron Saint)* and with all the Saints, on whose constant intercession in your presence we rely for unfailing help.

May this Sacrifice of our reconciliation, we pray, O Lord, advance the peace and salvation of all the world. Be pleased to confirm in faith and charity your pilgrim Church on earth, with your servant N. our Pope and N. our Bishop, the Order of Bishops, all the clergy, and the entire people you have gained for your own.

Listen graciously to the prayers of this family, whom you have summoned before you: in your compassion, O merciful Father, gather to yourself all your children scattered throughout the world.

To our departed brothers and sisters and to all who were pleasing to you at their passing from this life, give kind admittance to your kingdom. There, we hope to enjoy forever the fullness of your glory through Christ our Lord, through whom you bestow on the world all that is good.

* DOXOLOGY

P. Through him, and with him, and in him, O God, almighty Father, in the Unity of the Holy Spirit, all glory and honor is yours, forever and ever. -Amen

COMMUNION RITES

* OUR FATHER

P.- At the Savior's command and formed by divine teaching, we dare to say:

Our Father...

P.- Deliver us, Lord, we pray, from every evil, graciously grant peace in our days, that, by the help of your mercy, we may be always free from sin and safe from all distress, as we await the blessed hope and the coming of our Savior, Jesus Christ.

P.- For the kingdom, the power, and the glory are yours now and forever.

*** RITE OF PEACE**

P.- Lord Jesus Christ, you said to your apostles: Peace I leave you, my peace I give you, look not on our sins, but on the faith of your church, and graciously grant her peace and unity in accordance with your will. Who live and reign forever and ever.

P.- Amen.

P.- The peace of the Lord be with you always.

P.- And with your spirit.

P.- Let us offer each other the sign of peace.

BREAD FRACTION

Lamb of God, you take away the sins of the world, **Have mercy on us.**
Lamb of God, you take away the sins of the world, **Have mercy on us.**
Lamb of God, you take away the sins of the world, **Grant us peace.**
(The Priest shows the Holy Host on high)

P.- Behold the Lamb of God, behold him who takes away the sins of the world. Blessed are those called to the supper of the Lamb.

P.- Lord, I am not worthy that you should enter under my roof, but only say the word and my soul shall be healed.

COMMUNION

*** MOMENTS OF SILENCE OR PRAISE SONGS**

All those who are properly disposed and prepared come forward for communion and approach the priest who gives them communion saying:

P.- The Body of Christ,
Faithful: Amen.

*** THANKSGIVING.**
(It is necessary that all those who have received Holy Communion give thanks for a few minutes for this great gift they carry in their souls).

*** PRAYER AFTER COMMUNION**
S.- Let us pray... For Jesus Christ our Lord.
P.- Amen

<u>GREETINGS AND FAREWELL</u>   STANDING

Then, the farewell takes place. The priest extends his hands to the people and says:

P.- The Lord be with you.

P.- And with your spirit.

BLESSING:

P.- May Almighty God bless you, the Father, and the Son, and the Holy Spirit.
P.- Amen.

Go forth, the Mass is ended.

Thanks be to God.

<u>CHRISTIAN PRAYERS</u>

<u>(7) USUAL PRAYERS</u>

<u>SIGN OF THE CROSS</u>

By the sign + of the Holy Cross, from our + enemies deliver us Lord, + our God. In the name of the Father, + and of the Son, and of the Holy Spirit. Amen.

<u>OUR FATHER</u>

Our Father, who art in heaven, hallowed be thy name; thy kingdom come; thy will be done, on earth as it is in heaven. Give us this day our daily bread and forgive us our trespasses, as we forgive those who trespass against us, and lead us not into temptation, but deliver us from evil. Amen.

GLORY TO THE FATHER

Glory be to the Father, and to the Son, and to the Holy Spirit. As it was in the beginning, now and forever, and forever and ever. Amen.

CREED

I believe in God, the Father almighty, Creator of heaven and earth. I believe in Jesus Christ, his only Son, our Lord, who was conceived by the power and grace of the Holy Spirit, was born of the Virgin Mary, suffered under Pontius Pilate, was crucified, died and was buried, descended into hell, on the third day rose again from the dead, ascended into heaven, and is seated at the right hand of God, the Father almighty. From there he will come to judge the living and the dead. I believe in the Holy Spirit, the holy catholic Church, the communion of saints, the forgiveness of sins, the resurrection of the body, and the life everlasting. Amen.

I CONFESS

I confess before Almighty God and before you, my brethren, that I have sinned much in thought, word, deed and omission. Through my fault, through my fault, through my most grievous fault. Therefore I pray to the ever-virgin Mary, to the angels, to the saints and to you, my brothers and sisters, to intercede for me before God our Lord.

ACT OF CONTRITION

My Lord, Jesus Christ! God and true Man, my Creator, Father and Redeemer; because You are who You are, infinite Goodness, and because I love You above all things, I am heartily sorry that I have offended You; I am also sorry because You can punish me with the pains of hell. With the help of your divine grace, I firmly resolve never again to sin, to go to confession and to fulfill the penance imposed on me. Amen.

HAIL MARY

Hail Mary, full of grace, the Lord is with thee; blessed art thou among women, and blessed is the fruit of thy womb, Jesus. Holy Mary, Mother of God, pray for us sinners, now and at the hour of our death. Amen.

THE HAIL

Hail, Queen and Mother of mercy, our life, our sweetness and our hope. Hail God. To thee do we call, the banished children of Eve; to thee do we sigh, groaning and weeping in this vale of tears. O our advocate, turn to us your merciful eyes, and after this exile, show us Jesus, the blessed fruit of your womb. O clement, O merciful, O sweet Virgin Mary! Pray for us, O holy Mother of God, that we may be worthy to attain the promises of our Lord Jesus Christ. Amen.

REMEMBER

Remember, O most pious Virgin Mary, that never has it been heard that any of those who have come to your protection imploring your presence and claiming your help, have been forsaken by you. Encouraged by this confidence, I also come to you, O Virgin Mother and Mother of virgins, and groaning under the weight of my sins, I dare to appear before your sovereign presence. O Mother of God, do not reject my humble supplications, but rather incline your help to them and deign to attend to them favorably. Amen.

BLESSED BE YOUR PURITY

Blessed be your purity and eternally so, for a whole God is recreated in such great precious beauty, to you celestial princess, sacred Virgin Mary I offer you on this day, soul, life and heart. Look upon me with compassion, do not leave me, my Mother. Amen.

GUARDIAN ANGEL

Guardian Angel, sweet companion, do not forsake me, night or day, do not leave me alone because I would lose myself. Amen.

PRAYER OF ST. THÉRÈSE OF AVILA

Let nothing disturb you: let nothing frighten you.
All things pass away. God does not change.
Patience is all-sufficient.
He who has God lacks nothing.
God alone is enough. Amen.

PRAYER FOR PURITY

O guardian and father of virgins, St. Joseph, to whose faithful custody were entrusted the same innocence, Christ Jesus, and the Virgin of virgins Mary, by these two dearest garments, Jesus and Mary, I beg and beseech you to obtain for me that, preserved from all impurity, I may always serve Jesus and Mary with a clean soul, pure heart and chaste body. Amen.

<u>COME, HOLY SPIRIT (for Bible or Spiritual Reading)</u>

<u>Before:</u>

V. Come, Holy Spirit, fill the hearts of your faithful and kindle in them the fire of your love. Send forth your Spirit and all will be created.

R. And you will renew the face of the earth.

O God, who hast instructed the hearts of thy faithful with the light of the Holy Spirit, grant that we may feel rightly with the same Spirit and always enjoy his divine consolation. Through Jesus Christ our Lord. Amen.

<u>After:</u>

V. We thank you, almighty God, for all your benefits. Who livest and reignest for ever and ever.
R. Amen.

MENTAL PRAYER

Before

My Lord and my God, I firmly believe that you are here, that you see me, that you hear me; I adore you with profound reverence, I ask you for forgiveness of my sins, and grace to make this time of prayer fruitful. My Immaculate Mother, St. Joseph, my Father and Lord, my guardian Angel, intercede for me.

After

I thank You, my God, for the good intentions, affections and inspirations that You have communicated to me in this meditation; I ask Your help to put them into action. My Immaculate Mother, St. Joseph, my Father and Lord, my guardian Angel, intercede for me.

TABLE BLESSING

Before:

V. Bless us, + Lord, and bless this food that by your goodness we are about to take. Through Jesus Christ our Lord...

R. Amen.

(Add at noon and in the afternoon)

V. May the King of Glory make us partakers of the heavenly table.

R. Amen.

After:

V. We thank you, Lord, for all your benefits. You who live and reign forever and ever.

R. Amen.

V. May the Lord give us His peace.+

R. And eternal life. Amen.

ANGELUS (Midday Prayer)

D.- The Angel of the Lord announced to Mary.

R.- And she conceived by the power and grace of the Holy Spirit.

D.- Hail Mary...

R.- Saint Mary...

D.- Behold the handmaid of the Lord..

R.- Let it be done to me according to your Word.

D.- Hail Mary...

D.- The Son of God became man.

R.- And He dwelt among us.

D.- Hail Mary...

D.- Pray for us, Holy Mother of God.

R.- That we may be worthy to attain the promises of our Lord Jesus Christ.

D.- Prayer: We beseech you Lord to pour your grace into our souls, so that those of us who, through the angel's announcement, have known the incarnation of your Son Jesus Christ, by the merits of his passion and his Cross, may be brought to the glory of the Resurrection. Through the same Christ our Lord.

R.- Amen.

REGINA COELI

D.- Rejoice, full of grace. Alleluia.

R.- For he whom you deserved to carry in your bosom. Alleluia.

D.- He is risen, as predicted. Alleluia.

R.- Pray for us to God. Alleluia.

D.- Rejoice and be glad, Virgin Mary. Alleluia.

R.- For he is risen, God indeed. Alleluia.

D.- Let us pray: O God who by the admirable resurrection of our Lord Jesus Christ, hast deigned to give joy to the world, grant that through the intercession of his Mother, we may attain the joys of eternal Life. Through the same Christ our Lord.

R.- Amen.

JACULATORIES

The ejaculatories are short vocal prayers that help to maintain the presence of God throughout the day. Memorize them and say them when you go to the countryside, to see your animals, on a trip... everywhere.

Create in me, O God, a pure heart.

A contrite and humbled heart, O God, You do not despise.

To God all glory.

To those who love God, all is for the best.

For You, O God, are my strength.

It is fitting that He should increase and I should decrease.

Here I am, for you have called me.

Holy Mary, our hope, seat of wisdom, pray for us.

Holy Mary, our hope, handmaid of the Lord, pray for us.

Holy Mary, star of the East, help your children.

I can do all things in him who comforts me.

I believe, O Lord, but help my unbelief.

I thank Thee for all Thy benefits, even for those who are not known.

In Thee, O God, I trust; let me never be confounded.

Jesus, Son of David, have mercy on me, a sinner!

Jesus, Jesus, be for me always, Jesus.

Lord, Thou knowest all things, Thou knowest that I love Thee.

Lord, may I see, increase our faith!

Lord, what do You want me to do?

Holy Mary, Mother of the beautiful love, help your children.

My Lord and my God!

(8) MORNING PRAYERS

OFFERING OF THE DAY

Lord Jesus, through the Immaculate Heart of Mary, our Mother, I consecrate myself to your heart and with you to the Father, through the Holy Spirit, in your Holy Sacrifice of the Altar, with my prayer and my work, sufferings, and joys of today, in reparation for our sins. And that your kingdom may come to us. I ask you, especially for the Pope and the intentions he has entrusted this month to the Apostleship of Prayer. Amen.

TO MAINTAIN THE PRESENCE OF THE LORD

Lord, almighty God, who hast brought us to the beginning of this day; save us this day by thy power, that we may not fall into any sin; but that our words, thoughts, and actions may follow the way of thy commandments. Through our Lord Jesus Christ, your Son, who lives and reigns with you, in the unity of the Holy Spirit, forever and ever. Amen.

PRAYERS OF THANKSGIVING
FOR THE HOLY MASS AND COMMUNION

SOUL OF CHRIST

Soul of Christ, sanctify me. Body of Christ, save me. Blood of Christ, inebriate me. Water from the side of Christ, wash me. Passion of Christ, comfort me. O good Jesus, hear me. Within your wounds, hide me. Do not allow me to turn away from You. From the evil enemy, defend me. In the hour of my death, call me. And command me to come to Thee. That with Thy saints I may praise Thee. Forever and ever. Amen.

ACT OF DELIVERY OF YES

Take, O Lord, and receive my liberty, my memory, my understanding, and all my will, all that I have and possess. Thou gavest it to me; to Thee, O Lord, I give it; all is Thine; dispose of it according to Thy will. Give me your love and grace, for this is enough for me. Amen.

PRAYER OF SAINT FRANCISCO

Lord, You are everything, and I am nothing. You are the Creator of all things, You who preserves the whole universe, and I am nothing. Lord, make me an instrument of your peace. Where there is hatred, let me sow love; where there is injury, pardon; where there is doubt, faith; where there is sadness, joy; where there is discouragement, hope; where there is darkness, your light. O Divine Master, may I not seek to be consoled, but to console; may I not seek to be loved, but to love; may I not seek to be understood, but to understand; forgiving is how you receive us; forgiving is how you forgive us; and dying in you is how we are born to eternal life.

PRAYER BEFORE THE CRUCIFIX

Look at me, O my beloved and good Jesus! Prostrate me in your presence; I beg you with the greatest fervor to imprint in my heart lively sentiments of faith, hope, and charity, true sorrow for my sins, and the firmest resolution never to offend you; while I, who am capable, with the greatest affection and compassion consider and contemplate your five wounds, keeping in mind what the Prophet David said of you, O good Jesus: "They have pierced my hands and my feet and all my bones can be counted" (Ps. 22: 16-18).

PRAYER TO THE MOST HOLY VIRGIN

O Mary, Virgin, and Most Holy Mother, I have received your most beloved Son, whom you conceived in your immaculate womb, raising him and nourishing him at your breast, and you lovingly embraced him in your arms. The same Son whom you were happy to contemplate and filled you with joy; with love and humility, I present him to you and offer him to you so that you may embrace him, love him with your heart, and offer him to the Most Holy Trinity in supreme worship of adoration, for your honor and for your glory and for my needs and for those of the whole world. I beg you, most pious Mother, to obtain for me the forgiveness of my sins and abundant grace to serve you, from now on, with greater fidelity; and finally, the grace of final perseverance, so that I may praise him with you forever and ever. Amen.

PRAYER TO SAINT JOSEPH

Custodian and father of virgins, St. Joseph, to whose faithful custody were entrusted the same innocence, Christ Jesus, and the Virgin of virgins, Mary. By these two dearest garments, Jesus and Mary, I beg and beseech Thee to obtain for me that, preserved from all impurity, I may always serve Jesus and Mary with a clean soul, pure heart, and chaste body. Amen.

VISIT TO THE BLESSED SACRAMENT

(Three times the same)
D.- May he be forever blessed and praised.
R.- Jesus in the Blessed Sacrament
Our Father, Hail Mary and Glory Be
(A fourth time)
D.- May he be forever blessed and praised.
R.- Jesus in the Blessed Sacrament
Spiritual communion: **I would like, Lord, to receive you with that purity, humility, and devotion with which your Blessed Mother received you, with the spirit and fervor of the Saints.**

BLESSING WITH THE BLESSED SACRAMENT

S.- You gave them, bread from heaven.
R.- That it contains, yes, all delight.
S.- O God, who in this Sacrament admirably left us the memorial of your Passion, we ask you to venerate in such a way the mystery of your Body and Blood that we may constantly experience in us the fruit of your redemption. You who live and reign forever and ever.
R.- Amen.
(Then the priest blesses those present with the Blessed Sacrament)

<u>(9) HOW TO MAKE A GOOD CONFESSION?</u>

"Be prepared for a proper reconciliation to be made."

The basic requirement for making a good confession is to have **the intention to return to God** like the prodigal son and to acknowledge our sins with true contrition before his representative, the priest.

"An indispensable condition is, first of all, the uprightness and transparency of the penitent's conscience. A man does not set out on the path of true and genuine penance until he discovers that sin contrasts with the ethical norm, inscribed in the intimacy of his own being; until he acknowledges having had the personal experience and being responsible for such a contrast; until he does not say only that 'sin exists,' but 'I have sinned'; until he admits that sin has introduced into his conscience a division that invades his whole being and separates him from God and from his brothers."

The five requirements for a good confession are the following:

1° Examination of Conscience: To review the acts since the last confession. Well done.

2° Sorrow for sins: It is the contrition or sorrow for having offended God or the neighbor.

3° Purpose of amendment: It is the decision of not committing those sins again.

4° To tell the sins to the confessor: The mortal and venial sins must be told. All of them.

5° Fulfill the penance imposed: The prayers indicated by the confessor are prayed.

<u>EXAMINATION OF CONSCIENCE</u>

Examine your conscience.

You remember your sins by asking yourself without haste what you have done against the commandments of the Law of God and of the Church, with full warning and full consent.

<u>FIRST COMMANDMENT</u>

Have I seriously admitted any doubt against the truths of the faith? Have I come to deny the faith or some of its truths in my thoughts or before others?

Have I despaired of my salvation or abused my confidence in God, presuming that He would not abandon me in order to sin with greater ease?

Have I internally or externally disowned the Lord when some misfortune has befallen me?

Have I abandoned the holy Mass or the recitation of the Rosary, which are necessary for salvation? Have I tried to know my Catholic religion better?

Have I spoken without reverence of holy things, of the sacraments, of the Church, of her ministers?

Have I dealt with witchcraft, harm, horoscopes, or card-reading?

Have I unworthily received any sacrament?

Have I read or withheld books, magazines, or newspapers that go against faith or morals? Have I given them to others to read?

Do I participate in parish celebrations and formation activities?

SECOND COMMANDMENT

Have I blasphemed or blasphemed in front of others?

Have I made any vows, oaths, or promises and failed to keep them because of me?

Have I honored God's holy name? Have I pronounced God's name disrespectfully, angrily, mockingly, or in any other disrespectful way?

If I have overheard words or conversations against God, have I asked forgiveness for these sins?

Have I sworn untruthfully, unnecessarily, unwisely, or for something of little consequence?

THIRD COMMANDMENT TO THE 4 COMMANDMENTS OF THE CHURCH

Do I believe all that the Catholic Church teaches, and do I ignore her commands, forgetting that they are Christ's commands?

Have I missed Mass on Sundays or Holy Days of Obligation? Was it my fault? Have I been distracted voluntarily, or have I arrived so late that I have not complied with the precept?

Have I kept the fast one hour before the time of Communion?

Have I worked or had work done without urgent necessity on a day of obligation, in activities that prevent the worship due to God or the necessary rest of spirit and body?

Have I observed abstinence during the Fridays of Lent?

Have I said any prayer or performed any act of penance on the other Fridays of the year when I have not observed abstinence? Have I fasted and observed abstinence on Ash Wednesday and Good Friday? Did I fulfill the penance imposed on me by the priest at my last confession? Have I done penance for my sins? Have I gone to confession at least once a year? Have I kept silent in confession, out of shame, about some grave sin? Have I ever taken communion afterwards?

FOURTH COMMANDMENT
(Children)

Have I disobeyed my parents or superiors in important things?

Have I saddened them with my conduct? Am I disobedient?

Have I threatened or mistreated them by word or deed, or have I wished them any serious or slight harm?

Have I been responsible to my parents for the effort they make for my education, studying hard?

Have I failed to help them in their spiritual or material needs?

Do I let my temper get the better of me and get angry frequently and without a justified reason?

Am I selfish with the things I have, and it hurts me to leave them to the other brothers?

Have I quarreled with my siblings?

Have I stopped talking to them, and have I not taken the necessary steps for reconciliation?

Am I envious and it hurts me that others surpass me in some aspect?

Have I set a bad example to my brothers?

(Parents)

Do I disobey my superiors in important matters?

Do I remain indifferent to the needs, problems, and sufferings of the people around me, especially those who are close to me, for reasons of coexistence or work? Am I a cause of sadness for my co-workers because of negligence, discourtesy, or bad character?

Have I set a bad example to my children by not fulfilling my religious, family, or professional duties? Have I made them sad by my conduct? Have I abused my authority and ascendancy by forcing my family to receive the sacraments without thinking that out of shame or human excuse, they could do so without the proper dispositions?

Have I prevented my children from following the vocation with which God calls them to his service? Have I put obstacles in their way, or have I given them bad advice?

In guiding my children in their professional formation, have I been guided by objective reasons of ability and means, or have I followed the dictates of my vanity or selfishness?

Have I opposed their marriage without reasonable cause?

Have I tolerated scandals or moral or physical dangers among the people living in my house?

Have I sacrificed my tastes, whims, and amusements to fulfill my duty of dedication to the family?

Do I try to make friends with my children? Have I been able to create a climate of familiarity while avoiding responsibility?

Do I do my best to overcome the routine in my affection for my spouse?

Have I quarreled with my spouse? Have there been mistreatments in word or deed? Have I strengthened my spouse's authority, avoiding reprimanding, contradicting, or arguing with him/her in front of the children? Have I disobeyed or insulted him/her? Have I set a bad example?

Have I complained in front of the family about the burden of domestic duties? Have I left my spouse alone for too long?

Have I tried to revive my faith in Providence and earn enough to be able to have or educate more children?

FIFTH COMMANDMENT

Do I try to avoid enmity, hatred, or resentment towards someone?

Have I stopped talking to someone and refused to reconcile, or do not do my best to achieve reconciliation?

Do I avoid letting cultural or economic differences lead to hatred toward people?

Have I wished a serious evil on my neighbor, and have I rejoiced in the evils that have befallen him/her?

Have I let myself be dominated by envy, or do I not look well on some relatives or friends?

Have I allowed myself to be carried away by anger and bad words, reneging?

Have I despised my neighbor? Have I made fun of others, or have I criticized, teased, or ridiculed them?

Have I mistreated others by word or deed? Have I asked for things with bad manners, lacking in charity?

Have I hurt or taken the life of others?

Have I practiced or collaborated in the performance of an abortion? Have I aborted or induced someone to abort, knowing that it constitutes a very grave sin that carries with it ex-communication?

By my conversation, my manner of dress, my invitation to attend a show, or by lending a book or magazine, have I caused others to sin? Have I tried to repair the scandal?

Have I neglected my health? Have I made an attempt against my life? Have I been drunk, drunk to excess, or taken drugs?

Have I been drunk, drunk to excess, or taken drugs? Have I let myself be dominated by gluttony, that is, by the pleasure of eating and drinking beyond what is reasonable?

Have I cared for the good of my neighbor, warning him of the material or spiritual danger he is in or correcting him as required by Christian charity?

Have I neglected my work, failing to do justice in important things? Am I willing to repair the damage that has resulted from my negligence?

Do I try to finish the work well, thinking that God should not be offered things badly done?

Do I encourage problems of inheritance, boundaries, misuse of water, or neglect of the animals to damage the pastures of the neighbors?

Do I often delay the moment to start working or studying?

Have I, out of laziness, allowed serious damage to occur in my work? Have I neglected my performance in important things to the detriment of those for whom I work?

SIXTH AND NINTH COMMANDMENTS

Have I entertained myself with dishonest thoughts or memories? Have I brought to my memory impure memories or thoughts?

Have I let myself be carried away by evil desires against the virtue of purity, even if I did not act on them? Were there any circumstances that aggravated them: kinship, marriage, or consecration to God in the persons to whom they were directed?

Have I had impure conversations, or have I started them?

Have I attended entertainments that put me in close occasion of sinning (certain parties or immoral spectacles, bad readings or companies)? Do I realize that to put myself on those occasions is already a sin?

Have I entertained myself with impure glances? Have I rejected impure sensations? Have I done impure actions?

Have I done impure actions? Alone or with other people? How many times? Of the same or different sex? Was there any circumstance of kinship or affinity that gave it special gravity? Did these relationships have consequences? Did I do something to prevent them? After the new life was formed? Do I have friendships that are habitual occasions of sin? Am I willing to leave them?

***In courtship,** is true love its fundamental reason? Do I live the constant and joyful sacrifice of not turning affection into an occasion of sin?

The engagement should be an occasion to deepen affection and mutual knowledge; do I try to avoid a desire for possession, practicing the spirit of self-giving, understanding, respect, and delicacy?

Do I approach more frequently the sacrament of Penance during the engagement in order to have more grace from God?

***(Spouses)**

Have I misused marriage? Have I denied the other spouse his or her right? Have I violated marital fidelity by desire or deed? Have I used marriage only on those days when there can be no offspring?

Do I make use of marriage only on those days when there can be no offspring? Do I follow this mode of birth control without serious reasons?

Have I used condoms or taken drugs to avoid children? Have I induced others to take them?

<u>SEVENTH AND TENTH COMMANDMENTS</u>

Have I stolen anything, animal or amount of money? Have I repaired or restituted when I could have done so? Am I willing to do so? Have I cooperated with others in any theft or robbery? Were there any circumstances that aggravated it, for example, if it was a sacred object?

Have I retained what belongs to others against the will of its owner?

Have I harmed others by deceit, trickery, or coercion in contracts or business relationships?

Have I otherwise damaged their property, for example, their crops or animals? Have I cheated by overcharging? Have I repaired the damage caused, or do I intend to do so?

Have I spent more than my position allows on liquor or the vices of roosters, cards, etc.?

Have I failed to give what is convenient to help the Church? Do I give alms according to my economic position?

Do I unduly withhold or delay the payment of chores or salaries?

In the performance of public offices or functions, have I allowed myself to be carried away by favoritism, favoritism of persons, and lack of justice?

Have I accurately fulfilled my social duties, e.g., payment of social insurance to my employees?

Have I paid the taxes that are fair?

<u>EIGHTH COMMANDMENT</u>

Have I told lies? Have I made reparation for any damage that may have resulted? Do I usually lie because it is in things of little importance?

Have I discovered, without just cause, serious defects in another person, even if they are true but not known? Have I made amends in some way, e.g., by speaking positively of that person?

Have I slandered by attributing to others what was not true? Have I repaired the damage, or am I willing to do so? Have I stopped defending the defamed or slandered neighbor? Have I made rash judgments against the neighbor? Have I allowed myself to be carried away by gossip?

Have I revealed important secrets of others, uncovering them without just cause? Have I repaired the damage done?

Have I spoken ill of other people or institutions on the sole basis that "they told me" or "the word on the street"? In other words, have I cooperated in this way to slander and backbiting?

Do I take into account that political, professional, or ideological discrepancies should not obfuscate me to the point of judging or speaking ill of others and that these differences do not authorize me to discover their moral defects unless the common good demands it?

Have I revealed secrets without just cause? Have I made use of personal gain of what I knew through official silence? Have I repaired the damage I caused by my actions?

BEFORE CONFESSION

ACT OF CONTRITION

My Lord, Jesus Christ! God and true Man, my Creator, Father, and Redeemer; because You are who You are, infinite Goodness, and because I love You above all things, I am heartily sorry for having offended You; I am also sorry because You can punish me with the pains of hell. With the help of your divine grace, I firmly propose never again to sin, to confess, and to fulfill the penance imposed on me. Amen.

CONFESSION OF SINS

You may begin with the sign + of the Cross and greet the priest with:

Forgive me, Father, my last confession was... (how many days, months, or years ago?)

• The sins that can be remembered are said, starting with the most serious ones.

• If you have doubts, feel embarrassed, or do not know how to confess, tell the priest.

• If you do not remember any mortal sin, it is good to confess at least some venial sins, saying at the end: "**I repent of all the sins of my past life, especially...** (mention here in a general way some sin for which you are particularly sorry, for example, against charity or chastity). (mention here in a general way some sin for which one is particularly sorry, for example, against charity or chastity)".

• The priest **will give us penance** and some advice that will help us to be better Christians.

• Then it is said, **"Lord Jesus, Son of God, have mercy on me who am a sinner (or: "... that I have sinned)"**

• The words of absolution are now listened to attentively, answering at the end: "**Amen**". Penance should be completed as soon as possible.

<u>AFTER CONFESSION</u>

Thank God for having forgiven you again. If later you remember some mortal sin that you have not confessed, you can be sure that it has also been forgiven, but you must say so at the next confession.

<u>(10) DEVOTIONS TO THE MOST BLESSED TRINITY</u>

<u>PRAYER TO THE TRINITY</u>

O Eternal Father, who willed to manifest your omnipotence in the Saints by their prodigies and virtues and by their fortitude in the use of their lives in your service: grant that we may know how to overcome with constancy all temptations and that never, during our life, sin may keep us away from you. Our Father, Hail Mary, and Glory Be.

O only-begotten Son, who willed to manifest your infinite wisdom in the Saints, communicating to them your inspirations and your light so that they may penetrate the divine truths and live a life of faith; grant that we, with your grace and help, may practice all the virtues and grow each day in holiness and perfection. Our Father, Hail Mary and Glory Be.

O Holy Spirit, who willed to manifest the unction of your love in the Saints, pouring upon their souls your gifts and your fruits, and inflaming them with zeal and charity: grant that we may know how to love ourselves, O God of love, above all things, and our neighbor as ourselves, without ever failing in charity for anything. Our Father, Hail Mary and Glory Be.

<u>PRAYER TO THE HOLY SPIRIT TO OBTAIN THE SEVEN GIFTS</u>

O Holy Spirit, sweet guest of the soul, grant me the gift of WISDOM, that I may aspire to eternal goods, UNDERSTANDING, that I may enlighten my mind with divine light, COUNSEL, that I may guide others along the way of salvation, STRENGTH, that I may bear the cross of each day, KNOWLEDGE, that I may know God and myself, PITY, that I may gladly serve the work of God, HOLY FEAR, that I may avoid offending you.

(11) DEVOTIONS TO OUR LORD JESUS CHRIST

Jesus Christ, having entered once for all into the sanctuary of heaven, intercedes unceasingly for us as the mediator at the right hand of the Father, who assures us permanently of the outpouring of the Holy Spirit. There is no other way to the Father except through Jesus Christ.

FIRST FRIDAY DEVOTION
TO THE SACRED HEART OF JESUS

Devotion to the Sacred Heart of Jesus is very ancient in the Church; however, it was St. Margaret Mary dé Alacoque who popularized it. Jesus appeared to her during the octave of the feast of Corpus Christi and said:

"Look at this heart of mine which, in spite of being consumed in burning love for men, receives from Christians nothing but sacrilege, contempt, indifference, and ingratitude, even in the very sacrament of my love. But what pierces my Heart most heartrendingly is that I receive these insults from persons consecrated especially to my service".

Our Lord made great promises to those who show him their love and make atonement for their own and others' sins: "I promise in the excessive mercy of my Heart, that my almighty love will grant to all those who receive communion on the first nine consecutive Fridays the grace of final perseverance: they will not die in my disgrace nor without receiving the Sacraments, my Heart becoming their safe haven at that last hour".

The great promise of the Sacred Heart of Jesus is very consoling: the grace of final perseverance and the joy of finding in his Most Sacred Heart a safe haven of mercy. To earn this grace, we must:

- Receive Holy Communion without interruption for nine consecutive First Fridays.
- Intend to honor the Sacred Heart of Jesus and to attain final perseverance.
- Offer each Holy Communion as an act of atonement for offenses committed against the Blessed Sacrament.

Pray before the Lord who looks at you, listens to you, and understands you here in His Temple

---

Prayer: O God, in the heart of your Son, wounded by our sins, you have deposited infinite treasures of charity; we ask that, in rendering him the homage of our love, we offer him a complete reparation. Through Jesus Christ our Lord. **Amen.**

<u>BIBLICAL READING</u> (Jn. 19: 31-37)

The Jews, because it was the day of the Parasceve, so that the bodies might not remain on the cross on the Sabbath, because it was a great Sabbath, begged Pilate to break their legs and take them away. So the soldiers came and broke the legs of the first and of the other who was crucified with him; but when they came to Jesus, when they saw him already dead, they did not break his legs, but one of the soldiers pierced his side with his spear, and immediately blood and water came out. He who saw it testifies, and his testimony is true; he knows that he speaks the truth so that you may believe; for this happened that the Scripture might be fulfilled, "You shall not break one of his bones." And another Scripture also says: "They shall look on him whom they have pierced".

THOUGHTS TO MEDITATE ON THE SURRENDER OF JESUS THE GOOD SHEPHERD

1. Love is revealed to us in the Incarnation, in the redemptive journey of Jesus Christ on our earth, up to the supreme sacrifice of the Cross, where it is manifested in a new sign: *one of the soldiers pierced Jesus' side with a spear, and immediately blood and water came out.* The water and blood of Jesus speak to us of a self-giving carried out to the last extreme, to the point of "all is finished," out of love. The fullness of God is revealed and given to us in Christ, in the love of Christ, in the Heart of Christ. For it is the Heart of the One *in whom dwells all the fullness of the divinity bodily.*

2. Let us keep in mind all the richness that is contained in these words: Sacred Heart of Jesus. When we speak of the human heart, we are not referring only to feelings, we are referring to the whole person who loves, who loves and treats others. And, in the way men express themselves, which the Holy Scriptures have collected so that we can understand divine things, the heart is considered as the summary and the source, the expression and the ultimate background of thoughts, words, and actions. A man is worth what his heart is worth, we can say in our language.

That is why, in dealing now with the Heart of Jesus, we are showing the certainty of God's love and the truth of his devotion to us. In recommending devotion to this Sacred Heart, we are recommending that we should direct ourselves entirely with all that we are: our soul, our feelings, our thoughts, our words and our actions, our works, and our joys to Jesus. This is what true devotion to the Heart of Jesus is all about knowing God and knowing ourselves, and looking to Jesus and turning to Him, who encourages us, teaches us, and guides us. There is no room in this devotion for more superficiality than that of a man who, not being fully human, does not succeed in perceiving the reality of God incarnate.

CONSECRATION TO THE SACRED HEART OF JESUS

St. Margaret Mary Alacoque

I give myself, and to the Sacred Heart of Our Lord Jesus Christ, I consecrate without reserve my person, my life, my works, my pains and sufferings. I commit myself to use no part of my being except to honor, love and glorify the Sacred Heart. This is my unchangeable purpose: to be entirely His and to do all things for His love. At the same time, I wholeheartedly renounce everything that displeases him. Sacred Heart of Jesus, I want to have you as the only object of my love. Be, then, my protector in this life and guarantee of eternal life. Be my strength in my weakness and inconstancy. Be propitiation and atonement for all the sins of my life. Heart full of goodness, be my refuge at the hour of my death and my intercessor before God the Father. Divert from me the chastisement of His just wrath. Heart of love, in You I put all my trust. From my wickedness, I fear all things. But from your Love, I hope all things. Eradicate from me, O Lord, all that displeases You or may turn me away from You. May your love be so deeply impressed in my heart that I may never forget you or be separated from you. My Lord and my Savior, I beseech Thee, by the love Thou hast for me, may my name be deeply engraved on Thy Sacred Heart; may my happiness and my glory be to live and die in Thy service. Amen.

LITANY OF THE SACRED HEART OF JESUS

Lord, have mercy on us. **Lord, have mercy on us.**

Christ, have mercy on us. **Christ, have mercy on us.**

Lord, have mercy on us. **Lord, have mercy on us.**

Christ, hear us. **Christ, hear us.**

Christ, listen to us. **Christ, listen to us.**

God, Heavenly Father. **Have mercy on us.**

God, Holy Spirit,

Holy Trinity, one God,

Heart of Jesus, Son of the Eternal Father,

Heart of Jesus, formed by the Holy Spirit in the womb of the Virgin Mary,

Heart of Jesus, formed by the Holy Spirit in the womb of the Virgin Mary.

Heart of Jesus, substantially united to the Word of God,

Heart of Jesus, of infinite majesty,

Heart of Jesus, holy temple of God,

Heart of Jesus, tabernacle of the Most High,

Heart of Jesus, house of God, and gate of heaven,

Heart of Jesus, burning bonfire of charity,

Heart of Jesus, asylum of justice and love,

Heart of Jesus, full of goodness and love,

Heart of Jesus, abyss of all virtues,

Heart of Jesus, worthy of all praise,

Heart of Jesus, King, and center of all hearts,

Heart of Jesus, in whom dwells all the treasures of wisdom and knowledge,

Heart of Jesus, in whom dwells all the Fullness of the divinity,

Heart of Jesus, in whom the Father has found his pleasure,

Heart of Jesus, from whose fullness we have all received,

Heart of Jesus, desire of the eternal hills,

Heart of Jesus, patient and of much mercy,

Heart of Jesus, rich for all who call upon you,

Heart of Jesus, source of life and holiness,

Heart of Jesus, propitiation for our sins,

Heart of Jesus, torn in pieces for our crimes,

Heart of Jesus made obedient unto death,

Heart of Jesus, pierced by a lance,

Heart of Jesus, our life and resurrection,

Heart of Jesus, our peace and our reconciliation,

Heart of Jesus, victim of sinners,

Heart of Jesus, salvation of those who hope in You,

Heart of Jesus, hope of those who die in You,

Heart of Jesus, delight of all saints,

Lamb of God, who takes away the sins of the world, **Forgive us, Lord.**

Lamb of God, who takes away the sins of the world, **Hear us, Lord.**

Lamb of God, who takes away the sins of the world, **Have mercy on us.**

Jesus, meek and humble of heart, **Make our hearts like Yours.**

Prayer: O God, when we contemplate the Heart of your beloved Son, we remember the benefits of his love for us; grant that we may receive from this divine source of grace more abundant gifts. Through Jesus Christ our Lord. **Amen.**

VIA CRUCIS

My Lord and my God

under the loving gaze of our Mother,

we are ready to accompany you

along the path of pain,

which was the price of our ransom.

We want to suffer all that you suffered,

to offer You our poor, contrite heart,

because you are innocent, and you are going to die for us,

who are the only guilty ones.

My Mother, sorrowful Virgin

help me to relive those bitter hours

that your Son wanted to spend on Earth,

so that we, made of a handful of mud,

might live at last

in the freedom and glory of the children of God.

I - STATION: JESUS IS CONDEMNED TO DEATH 

It is now past ten o'clock in the morning. The process is coming to an end. There has been no conclusive evidence. The judge knows that his enemies have given him up out of envy, and he tries an absurd resource: the choice between Barabbas, an evildoer accused of robbery with murder, and Jesus, who calls himself Christ. The people choose Barabbas. Pilate exclaims:

-What then shall I do with Jesus? (Mt. 27: 22).

They all answer: *-Crucify him!*

The judge insists: *-But what wrong has he done?*

And again, they shout back: *-Crucify him, crucify him!*

Pilate was frightened by the growing tumult. He then sends for water and washes his hands in the sight of the people while he says:

-I am innocent of the blood of this just man; you shall see (Mt. 27:24).

And after having Jesus scourged, he handed him over to be crucified. There is silence in those angry and possessed throats as if God were already defeated.

Jesus is alone. Long gone are those days when the word of the Man-God put light and hope in hearts, those long processions of the sick who were healed, the triumphant cries of Jerusalem when the Lord came riding on a gentle colt. If only men had wanted to give another course to the love of God! If you and I had known the day of the Lord!

II - STATION: JESUS IS BURDENED WITH THE CROSS 

Outside the city, northwest of Jerusalem, there is a small hill: Golgotha is called in Aramaic; locus Calvariae, in Latin: place of the Skulls or Calvary.

Jesus is delivered helplessly to the execution of the condemnation. Nothing is to be spared him, and the weight of the infamous cross falls on his shoulders. But the Cross will be, by the work of love, the throne of His kingship.

The people of Jerusalem and the strangers who have come for the Passover throng the streets of the city to see Jesus of Nazareth, the King of the Jews, pass by. There is a tumult of voices and, at intervals, short silences, perhaps when Christ fixes his eyes on someone:

- If anyone would come after me, let him take up his daily cross and follow me. (Mt. 16: 24).

With what love Jesus embraces, the log that is to put him to death!

Is it not true that as soon as you stop being afraid of the Cross, of what people call the cross, when you put your will to accept the divine Will, you are happy, and all worries, physical or moral sufferings pass away?

The Cross of Jesus is truly gentle and kind. There, sorrows do not count; only the joy of knowing that we are co-redeemers with Him.

III - STATION: JESUS FALLS BY THE WEIGHT OF THE CROSS 

The Cross cleaves shatters with its weight the shoulders of the Lord.

The crowd has been growing. The legionaries can hardly contain the angry, enraged crowd that, like a river out of course, flows through the narrow streets of Jerusalem.

The exhausted body of Jesus is already staggering under the enormous Cross. From His most loving Heart comes barely a breath of life to His wounded limbs.

On the right and on the left, the Lord sees this multitude walking like sheep without a shepherd. He could call them one by one, by their names, by our names. There are those who were fed at the multiplication of the loaves and fishes, those who were healed of their infirmities, those whom he indoctrinated by the lake and on the mountain and in the porches of the Temple.

A sharp pain penetrates the soul of Jesus, and the Lord collapses in exhaustion.

You and I can say nothing: now we know why the Cross of Jesus weighs so much. And we weep for our miseries and also for the tremendous ingratitude of the human heart. From the depths of our soul comes an act of true contrition, which lifts us out of the prostration of sin. Jesus has fallen so that we may rise up: once and for all time.

IV - STATION: JESUS MEETS HIS MOST HOLY MOTHER 

Scarcely has Jesus risen from his first fall when he meets his Blessed Mother, beside the road through which he is passing.

With immense love, Mary looks at Jesus, and Jesus looks at His Mother; their eyes meet, and each heart pours into the other its own sorrow. Mary's soul is flooded with bitterness, in the bitterness of Jesus Christ. O you who pass by the way, look and see if there is any sorrow like unto my sorrow (Lm. 1:12).

But no one notices, no one takes notice, only Jesus.

Simeon's prophecy has been fulfilled: *a sword will pierce your soul.*

(Lk. 2:35).

In the dark solitude of the Passion, Our Lady offers her Son a balm of tenderness, of union, of fidelity, a yes to the divine will.

From the hand of Mary, you and I also want to console Jesus, accepting always and in everything the Will of his Father, of our Father.

Only in this way will we taste the sweetness of the Cross of Christ and embrace it with the strength of love, carrying it in triumph along all the roads of the earth.

V - STATION: SIMON CYRENE HELPS JESUS  CARRY THE CROSS

Jesus is exhausted. His pace becomes more and more awkward, and the soldiers are in a hurry to finish; so, when they leave the city by the Judiciary Gate, they call for a man who came from a farm named Simon of Cyrene, father of Alexander and Rufus, and force him to carry the cross of Jesus (Mk. 15: 21).

In the Passion as a whole, this help is very little. But it is enough for Jesus to have a smile, a word, a gesture, and a little love to pour copiously his grace on the soul of the friend. Years later, Simon's sons, already Christians, will be known and esteemed among their brothers in the faith. It all began with an unexpected encounter with the Cross.

I appeared to those who did not ask for me, those who did not seek me found me (Is. 65:1).

Sometimes, the Cross appears without looking for it: it is Christ who asks for us. And if perhaps in the face of that unexpected Cross, and perhaps for that reason more obscure, the heart shows repugnance... do not give it consolations. And, full of noble compassion, when it asks for them, tell it slowly, as if in confidence: heart, heart on the Cross, heart on the Cross!

VI - STATION: A PIOUS WOMAN CLEANS THE FACE OF JESUS 

There is no appearance in him, no beauty to behold, no pleasing beauty. He is despised, the refuse of men, a man of sorrows, a knower of all destruction, to whom the face is turned away, despised, esteemed as nothing (Is. 53: 2-3).

And it is the Son of God who passes by, mad... mad with love!

A woman, Veronica by name, makes her way through the crowd, carrying a folded white cloth, with which she piously wipes the face of Jesus. The Lord leaves his Holy Face engraved on the three parts of the veil.

The beloved face of Jesus, who had smiled at the children and was transfigured with glory on Tabor, is now as it were hidden by sorrow. But this pain is our purification; that sweat and that blood that tarnishes and blurs his features, our cleansing.

Lord, may I decide to tear off, through penance, the sad mask that I have forged with my miseries.... Then, only then, by the path of contemplation and atonement, will my life faithfully copy the features of your life. We will become more and more like you.

We will be other Christs, the same Christ, *ipse Christus.*

VII - STATION: JESUS FALLS A SECOND TIME

Most Holy Humanity.

It was he who took upon himself our infirmities and bore our griefs, and we considered him punished, smitten by God, and humiliated. He was pierced for our iniquities and crushed for our sins. The chastisement of our salvation was upon him, and in his stripes we are healed (Is. 53:4-5).

Jesus fails, but his fall lifts us up. His death resurrects us.

To our backsliding in evil, Jesus responds with his insistence on redeeming us with an abundance of forgiveness. And, so that no one may despair, he again rises wearily embraced by the Cross.

May stumbles and defeats, which no longer keep us from him. As a weak child throws himself with compunction into the strong arms of his father, so shall you and I cling to the yoke of Jesus. Only this contrition and humility will transform our human weakness into divine strength.

VIII - STATION: JESUS COMFORTS THE DAUGHTERS OF 

JERUSALEM

Among the people contemplating the passing of the Lord, there are a few women who cannot contain their compassion and burst into tears, perhaps recalling those glorious days of Jesus Christ when all exclaimed in wonder: *bene omnia fecit* (Mk. 7:37), he has done all things well.

But the Lord wants to direct this weeping towards a more supernatural motive and invites them to weep for the sins which are the cause of the Passion and which will attract the rigor of divine justice:

-Daughters of Jerusalem, weep not for me, weep for yourselves and for your children..... For if the green tree is treated in this way, what will be done to the dry tree? (Lk. 23: 28-31).

Your sins, my sins, the sins of all men, stand up. All the evil we have done and the good we have failed to do. The desolate panorama of the untold crimes and infamies that we would have committed if He, Jesus, had not comforted us with the light of His most loving gaze.

How little is a life to repair!

IX - STATION: JESUS FALLS FOR THE THIRD TIME 

The Lord falls for the third time on the slope of Calvary when there are only forty or fifty steps left to reach the summit. Jesus does not stand upright: his strength is failing him, and he lies exhausted on the ground.

He gave Himself up because He wanted to; He was mistreated, He did not open His mouth, like a lamb led to the slaughter, like a sheep dumb before the shearers (Is. 53:7).

All against Him...: those of the city and the strangers, and the Pharisees and the soldiers and the chief priests...All executioners. His Mother - my Mother - Mary, weeps.

Jesus fulfills the will of his Father! Poor: naked. Generous: what remains for him to give? *Dilexit me, et tradidit semetipsum pro me* (Gal. 2:20), he loved me and gave himself up to death for me.

My God, may I hate sin and unite myself to You, embracing the Holy Cross, to fulfill in my turn Your most gracious Will..., naked of all earthly affection, with no other aim than Your glory..., generously, reserving nothing for myself, offering myself with You in perfect holocaust.

X - STATION: JESUS IS STRIPPED OF HIS GARMENTS 

When the Lord arrived at Calvary, he was given to drink a little wine mixed with gall, as a narcotic, to diminish somewhat the pain of the crucifixion. But Jesus, having tasted it in gratitude for this pious service, did not want to drink it (Mt. 27:34). He gives himself to death in the full freedom of love.

Then, the soldiers strip Christ of his clothes.

From the soles of his feet to his head, there is nothing healthy in him. Wounds, swellings, rotten sores, neither healed, nor bandaged, nor softened with oil (Is. 1:6).

The executioners take his garments and divide them into four parts. But the robe is seamless, so they say:

- *Let us not divide it; but let us cast lots to see whose it shall be* (Jn. 19:24).

Thus, the Scripture has been fulfilled once again: th*ey parted my garments among them and cast lots for my tunic* (Ps. 22:18-19).

It is the plundering, the plundering, the most absolute poverty. Nothing is left to the Lord but a wood.

To reach God, Christ is the way, but Christ is on the Cross, and to go up to the Cross, one must have a free heart, detached from the things of the earth.

XI - STATION: JESUS IS NAILED TO THE CROSS 

Now they crucify the Lord and beside Him two thieves, one on the right hand and one on the left. In the meantime, Jesus says:

-Father, forgive them, for they know not what they do (Lk. 23:34).

It is Love that brought Jesus to Calvary. And already on the Cross, all his gestures and all his words are of love, of serene and strong love.

With the gesture of an Eternal Priest, without father or mother, without genealogy (Heb. 7:3), he opens his arms to all humanity.

Together with the hammering of Jesus, the prophetic words of Holy Scripture resound: *they have pierced my hands and my feet. I can count all my bones, and they look upon me and behold me* (Ps. 22:16-18).

- *My people, what have I done unto thee, or wherein have I grieved thee? Answer me!* (Mi. 6:3).

And we, our souls broken with sorrow, sincerely say to Jesus: I am Yours, and I give myself to You, and I nail myself to the Cross gladly, being at the crossroads of the world a soul given to You, to Your glory, to the Redemption, to the damnation of all mankind.

XII - STATION: JESUS DIES ON THE CROSS 

On the top of the Cross is written the cause of condemnation: Jesus the Nazarene King of the Jews (Jn. 19:19). And all who pass by revil Him and mock Him.

- *If you are the king of Israel, come down now from the cross* (Mt. 27:42).

One of the thieves comes to His defense:

- *This one has done no wrong...* (Lk. 23:41).

Then he addresses to Jesus a humble petition, full of faith:

- *Lord, remember me when you are in your kingdom* (Lk. 23:42).

- *Truly I tell you, today you will be with me in paradise* (Lk. 23:43).

Next to the Cross is his Mother, Mary, with other holy women. Jesus looks at her, and then looks at the disciple he loves, and says to his Mother:

- *Woman, behold your son.*

Then he says to the disciple:

- *There you have your mother* (Jn. 19: 26-27).

The light of heaven is extinguished, and the earth is plunged into darkness. It was about three o'clock when Jesus exclaimed:

-Eli, Eli, lamma sabachtani?! That is, *My God, why hast thou forsaken me?* (Mt. 27:46).

Then, knowing that all things are about to be consummated so that the Scripture may be fulfilled, he says:

- *I thirst* (Jn. 19:28).

The soldiers soak a sponge in vinegar and putting it on a hyssop reed, put it to his mouth. Jesus sips the vinegar and exclaims:

- *All is accomplished* (Jn. 19:30).

The veil of the temple is rent, and the earth trembles when the Lord cries out with a loud voice:

- *Father, into thy hands I commend my spirit* (Lk. 23:46).

And He expires.

Love the sacrifice, which is the source of interior life. Love the Cross, which is the altar of sacrifice. Love pain, even to the point of drinking, like Christ, the dregs of the cup.

XIII - STATION: JESUS IS TAKEN DOWN FROM THE CROSS AND HANDED OVER TO HIS MOTHER ✝

Mary, overwhelmed with sorrow, is beside the Cross. And John, with her. But it is getting late, and the Jews urge that the Lord be taken away from there.

After having obtained from Pilate the permission required by Roman law to bury the condemned, *a senator named Joseph, a virtuous and just man, a native of Arimathea, arrives at Calvary. He has not consented to the condemnation, nor to what the others have executed.* On the contrary, he is one of those who hope in the kingdom of God (Lk. 23: 50-51). With him comes also Nicodemus, *the same one who on another occasion had gone by night to meet Jesus, and he brings with him a bundle of myrrh and aloes, about a hundred pounds* (Jn. 19:39).

They were not known publicly as disciples of the Master; they had not been found in the great miracles, nor did they accompany him in his triumphal entry into Jerusalem. Now, in the evil moment, when the others have fled, they are not afraid to stand up for their Lord.

Between the two of them, they take Jesus' body and leave him in the arms of his Blessed Mother. Mary's sorrow is renewed.

- *Where has your beloved gone, O most beautiful of women? Where has the one you love gone, and we will look for him with you?* (Sts. 6: 1-3).

The Blessed Virgin is our Mother, and we do not want to leave her alone.

XIV - STATION: THE BODY OF JESUS IS BURIED 

Very close to Calvary, in a garden, Joseph of Arimathea had a new tomb hewn out in the rock. And because it was the eve of the great Passover of the Jews, they put Jesus there. Then Joseph *rolled a great stone and shut the door of the tomb and went away* (Mt. 27:60).

Jesus came into the world with nothing, and with nothing - not even the place where he rests - he has left us.

The Mother of the Lord - my Mother - and the women who followed the Master from Galilee, after observing everything attentively, also leave. Night falls.

Now everything has passed. The work of our Redemption has been accomplished. We are now children of God because Jesus has died for us, and his death has redeemed us.

Empti enim estis pretio magno! (1 Cor. 6:20) You and I have been bought with a great price.

We are to make Christ's life and death our own. To die by mortification and penance so that Christ may live in us by Love. And then follow in the footsteps of Christ with the desire to co-redeem all souls.

To give one's life for others. This is the only way to live the life of Jesus Christ and become **one with Him.**

(12) DEVOTIONS TO THE HOLY VIRGIN

"All generations will call me blessed." The piety of the Church towards the Blessed Virgin is an intrinsic element of Christian worship. "The Blessed Virgin" is rightly honored by the Church with special worship. We do so now by means of the Holy Rosary.

HOLY ROSARY

The Holy Rosary is a very ancient devotion. Medieval piety in the West developed the prayer of the Rosary, replacing the Prayer of the Hours. It is a meditation on the life of Jesus Christ and the Virgin Mary. Christian prayer is preferably applied to meditate on 'the mysteries of Christ'.

- By the sign of the Holy Cross...

- My Lord, Jesus Christ...

V. Lord, open my lips, + R. And my mouth shall proclaim your praise.

V. My God, come to my aid!, + R. Lord, make haste to help me.

V. Glory be to the Father and to the Son and to the Holy Spirit.

R. As it was in the beginning, is now and ever shall be, forever and ever. Amen.

After announcing each mystery we pray an Our Father, ten Hail Marys, a Glory Be and **Mary, Mother of grace, Mother of mercy, defend us from our enemies and protect us now and at the hour of our death. Amen.**

Joyful Mysteries (Monday and Saturday)

1. The Incarnation of the Son of God.
2. The Visitation of the Virgin to her cousin St. Elizabeth.
3. The Birth of Jesus in Bethlehem.
4. The Presentation of the Child in the Temple.
5. The Child lost and found in the temple.

Luminous Mysteries (Thursday)

1. The Baptism of Jesus in the Jordan.
2. The Wedding at Cana.
3. Proclamation of the Kingdom and the need for conversion.
4. The Transfiguration of the Lord.
5. The Institution of the Holy Eucharist.

Sorrowful Mysteries (Tuesdays and Fridays)

1. The Prayer of Jesus in the Garden.
2. The Flagellation of the Lord.
3. The Crowning with thorns.
4. Jesus carrying the Cross.
5. Jesus dies on the Cross.

Glorious Mysteries (Wednesday and Sunday)

1. The Resurrection of the Lord.
2. The Ascension of the Lord.
3. The Coming of the Holy Spirit.
4. The Assumption of the Virgin Mary into Heaven.
5. The Coronation of Mary.

At the end of the five mysteries, we pray:

Hail Mary, Daughter of God the Father, full of...

Hail Mary, Mother of God the Son, full of...

Hail Mary, Bride of God the Holy Spirit, full of...

LAURETAN LITANIES

V. Lord, have mercy   **R. Lord, have mercy**

V. Christ, have mercy   **R. Christ, have mercy**

V. Lord, have mercy   **R. Lord, have mercy**

V. Christ, hear us   **R. Christ, hear us**

V. Christ, listen to us   **R. Christ, listen to us**

V. God, Heavenly Father   **R. Have mercy on us**

V. God the Son, Redeemer of the world   **R. Have mercy on us**

V. God Holy Spirit   **R. Have mercy on us**

V. Holy Trinity, one God   **R. Have mercy on us**

V. Holy Mary   **R.- Pray for us**

Holy Mother of God

Holy Virgin of virgins

Mother of Christ

Mother of the Church

Mother of divine grace

Mother most pure

Mother most chaste

Virgin Mother

Mother without stain

Immaculate Mother

Gentle Mother

Mother admirable

Mother of Good Counsel

Mother of the Creator

Mother of the Savior

Most prudent Virgin

Virgin worthy of veneration

Virgin worthy of praise

Most powerful Virgin

Clement Virgin

Faithful Virgin

Mirror of justice

Throne of wisdom

Cause of our joy

Spiritual vessel

Vessel worthy of honor

Vessel of devotion

Mystical rose

Tower of David

Ivory tower

House of gold

Ark of the covenant

Gate of heaven

Morning star

Health of the sick

Refuge of sinners

Comfort of the afflicted

Help of Christians

Queen of Angels

Queen of Patriarchs

Queen of Prophets

Queen of Apostles

Queen of Martyrs

Queen of Confessors

Queen of Virgins

Queen of all Saints

Queen conceived without original sin

Queen elevated to heaven

Queen of the Most Holy Rosary

Queen of the family

Queen of peace

V.   Lamb of God, who takes away the sins of the world.

R.   **Forgive us, Lord.**

V.   Lamb of God, who takes away the sins of the world.

R.   **Hear us, Lord.**

V.   Lamb of God, who takes away the sins of the world.

R.   **Have mercy on us.**

V. Under your protection we take refuge, Holy Mother of God: do not disregard our supplications that we address to you in our needs, but deliver us from danger, O glorious and blessed Virgin!
V. Pray for us, Holy Mother of God.
R. That we may be worthy to attain the promises of our Lord Jesus Christ.

Let us pray, we beseech you, Lord, to pour your grace into our souls so that we who, through the Angel's proclamation, have known the Incarnation of your Son Jesus Christ, through his Passion and Cross, may be brought to the glory of his Resurrection. Through the same Jesus Christ our Lord.
R. Amen.

- For the needs of the Church and the State: *Our Father, Hail Mary and Glory Be.*
- For the person and intentions of the Pope... and of our Bishop... *Our Father, Hail Mary and Glory Be.*
- For the increase and holiness of priestly and religious vocations and for the fidelity of priests. *Our Father, Hail Mary and Glory Be.*
- For the blessed souls in Purgatory: *Our Father, Hail Mary and may they rest in peace.* R. **Amen**.

(13) DEVOTIONS TO SAINT JOSEPH

PRAYER FOR EVERY DAY

Glorious Patriarch St. Joseph, animated by a great confidence in your great worth, I come to you to be my protector during the days of my exile in this valley of tears. Your very high dignity as the putative Father of my loving Jesus means that you will be denied nothing in heaven. Be my advocate, especially at the hour of my death, and obtain for me the grace that my soul, when it is detached from the flesh, may go to rest in the hands of the Lord. Amen.

Jaculatory. Most gracious St. Joseph, Spouse of Mary, protect us; defend the Church and the Supreme Pontiff and protect my relatives, friends and benefactors.

VISIT TO SAINT JOSEPH

O most chaste spouse of the Virgin Mary, my most loving protector St. Joseph! All who implore your protection experience your consolation. You, then, be my protection and my guide. Pray to the Lord for me; deliver me from sin, help me in temptations and keep me from evil and sin. Comfort me in sickness and affliction. May my thoughts, words and deeds be a faithful transcript of all that may be acceptable and pleasing to you, so that I may worthily deserve your protection in life and at the hour of death. Amen.

Jaculatory: O glorious St. Joseph! Make me constant in doing good; correct my faults and obtain for me the forgiveness of my sins.

PRAYER TO SAINT JOSEPH

St. Joseph, chaste spouse of the Virgin Mary, intercede for me to obtain the gift of purity.

You who, in spite of your personal insecurities, were able to docilely accept God's Plan as soon as you heard about it, help me to have the same attitude to respond always and everywhere to what the Lord asks of me.

Prudent man who did not cling to human securities but was always open to respond to the unexpected, obtain for me the help of the Divine Spirit so that I too may live in prudent detachment from earthly securities.

Model of zeal, of constant work, of silent fidelity, of paternal solicitude, obtain for me these blessings, so that I may grow more and more each day in them and thus resemble day by day the model of full humanity: THE LORD JESUS.

CONSECRATION TO SAINT JOSEPH IN THE FACE OF TRIBULATIONS

Hear, dear St. Joseph, a word from me! I am overwhelmed with afflictions and crosses, and I often weep..... Torn to pieces under the weight of these crosses, I feel faint, I do not have the strength to get up, and I wish that my God would call me soon. In tranquility, however, I understand that it is not difficult to die... but to live well. To whom, then, shall I turn but to You, who are so good and dear, to receive light... consolation... and help? To You, then, I consecrate my whole life, and into Your hands I place the sorrows, the crosses, the interests of my soul... of my family... of sinners... so that, after a life so laborious, we may go to enjoy forever with You the blessedness of Paradise. Amen.

Jaculatory. St. Joseph, Protector of the troubled and the dying, pray for us.

CONSECRATION TO SAINT JOSEPH

O Glorious Patriarch Saint Joseph, here I am, prostrate on my knees before your presence, to ask for your protection. I choose you as my father, protector and guide. Under your protection I place my body and soul, property, life and health. Accept me as your son. Preserve me from all dangers, snares and snares of the enemy. Assist me at all times and above all at the hour of my death. Amen.

By the sign of the Holy Cross...

Act of contrition.

<u>(14) DEVOTIONS TO THE SAINTS</u>

<u>PRAYER TO THE SAINT</u>

<u>IN WHOSE HONOR THE NOVENA IS HELD</u>

Glorious Saint, we come to you, full of confidence in your intercession. We are drawn to you with a special devotion and we know that our supplications will be more pleasing to God our Lord if you, who are so dear to Him, present them to Him. Your charity, an admirable reflection of God's, inclines you to help every misery, to console every sorrow and to satisfy every desire and need, if it will be beneficial to our soul. Look, then, upon our miseries and sorrows, our labors and necessities, our good desires, and obtain for us that we may secure our eternal salvation more and more each day by the practice of good works and the imitation of your virtues. And, in particular, we ask you to obtain for us from God the special grace which, by this devout novena, we confidently hope to obtain. So be it.

(Now we ask for the special grace that, through the Novena, we want to obtain).

<u>PRAYER TO GOD OUR LORD</u>

O God, You have willed to spread in a marvelous way, throughout all creation, reflections of Your uncreated beauty and infinite omnipotence, and You have created man to be a living image of You, in which You could take pleasure; so great is Your goodness and pleasure with the souls who love You from the heart and surrender themselves totally to You as do Your saints, whom You make participants of Your power, making them work prodigies and miracles. We beseech you today, since by our merits we do not deserve to be attended to, that you will listen to us through your goodness and through the worthiness of your glorious Saint, and that you will grant us the graces that through his mediation we ask of you in this novena. And now, trusting in your infinite goodness, we dare to insist on our supplications, while, prostrate, with the greatest respect and with all the affection of our heart, we address the following supplications to the Most Holy Trinity:

- **O Eternal Father**, who wished to manifest your omnipotence in the Saints by their prodigies and virtues and by their strength in the use of their lives in your service: grant that we may know how to overcome with constancy all temptations and that sin may never, during our life, keep us from you.

  Our Father, Hail Mary, and Glory Be.

- **O Only-Begotten Son**, who willed to manifest your infinite wisdom in the Saints, communicating to them your inspirations and your light, so that they may penetrate the divine truths and live a life of faith; grant that we, with your grace and help, may practice all the virtues and grow each day in holiness and perfection.

  Our Father, Hail Mary, and Glory Be.

- **O Holy Spirit**, who willed to manifest the unction of your love in the Saints, pouring your gifts and your fruits upon their souls, and inflaming them with zeal and charity: grant that we may know how to love you, O God of love, above all things, and our neighbor as ourselves, without ever failing in charity for anything.

- *Our Father, Hail Mary, and Glory Be.*

<u>CLOSING PRAYER</u>

O God of infinite Goodness. You have willed that your Saints should be for us not only powerful intercessors, but something more: that they should be our models. Of their virtues, the one we should imitate most is that of pure love and perfect union of will with You, our God and Lord. This virtue is the one that most unites us to you and makes us most holy. Let our poor offering, then, be this desire and resolution which we now again make to so unite our will with yours, that we may never will anything but what you will, and that we may resolutely cease to do whatever we know to be outside your divine and paternal will. Made in this spirit, our prayers will be more agreeable to you, and by conforming ourselves beforehand to all that you wish of us, we are more certain to obtain what we have asked of you.

V. The Saints will live forever.

R. And his reward is in the Lord.

Grant us the grace, O Lord, we beseech you, that through the intercession of Saint ..., whose virtues we venerate here on earth, we may one day be numbered with him/her in heaven. Through our Lord Jesus Christ, Amen.

PRAYERS FOR ANY SAINT

I

Glorious Saint... we come to you, full of confidence in your intercession. We are drawn to you with a special devotion and we know that our petitions will be more pleasing to God our Lord if you, who are so dear to Him, present them to Him. Your charity, an admirable reflection of God's, inclines you to help every misery, to console every sorrow and to satisfy every desire and need, if it will be to the benefit of our soul. Look, then, upon our miseries and sorrows, our labors and needs, our good desires, and obtain for us that each day we may secure more and more our eternal salvation by the practice of good works and the imitation of your virtues.

II

Almighty God, who has poured throughout creation reflections of your infinite beauty and goodness, making man in your image and likeness, you love so much those who give themselves totally that you put them as a model for us. You want us to venerate them and you do countless benefits and miracles through their intercession. For this reason and through your servant...we beg you to grant us (mention here the petition) and with it a greater correspondence to your love.

PRAYER TO THE SAINT OF OUR NAME

Saint... whom I truly love, and under whose special protection my beloved mother the Church has placed me by making me her child in baptism, I beg you not to cease, today or ever, to watch over me so that I may live as befits a Christian, and according to my name, following your example. Help me in my difficulties; above all, do not allow me to fall into sin, and grant that I may know how to make my life my greatest consolation at the hour of death, so that I may be eternally happy with you. Amen.

<u>PRAYER TO OUR PATRON SAINT</u>

Saint..., my patron and protector, divine providence placed me under your protection on the day of my baptism. I beg you to help me with your intercession, to live as befits a true Christian who has been honored with your enlightened name. Do not allow me to dishonor it with my bad actions; and I ask you to stimulate me to imitate your virtues, so that I may be able to accompany you in heaven. Amen.

(15) DEVOTIONS AT THE HOUR OF DEATH
TO OBTAIN A GOOD DEATH (Pray at any time)

O Creator and my Father, I implore from You the most important of all graces: final perseverance and a holy death. Although I have wasted much of the life You have given me so far, grant me the grace to live it well from this moment on and to end it in Your holy honor.

Grant me to die like the Holy Patriarchs, leaving this vale of tears without sorrow, to go and enjoy eternal rest in my true homeland.

Grant me to die like the glorious St. Joseph, accompanied by Jesus and Mary, pronouncing those most sweet names which I hope to extol eternally.

Grant me to die like the Immaculate Virgin, with the purest love and desiring to unite myself to my only love.

Grant that I may die like Jesus on the Cross, fully identified with the will of the Father and converted by love into a holocaust.

Lord Jesus, having accepted death for me, give me the grace to die in a perfect act of love for You.

Holy Mary, Mother of God, pray for me now and at the hour of my death.

St. Joseph, my father and lord, grant me to die as one of the righteous.

RECOMMENDATION OF THE SOUL

From baptism to death, the Christian's existence must be a continuous waiting for the Lord who is coming: "Yes, I am coming at once. Amen. Come, Lord Jesus" (Rev. 22:20). When the culminating moment of the encounter with the Lord arrives, that is to say, when the sick person reaches his last agony, he should be assisted by at least some of the faithful, presided over if possible by a priest or catechist, and accompanied in his passage by the prayer of the Church. For this purpose, *brief invocations, biblical readings and the litany of the saints* listed below may be used.

PRAYERS BEFORE THE DYING

1.- INVOCATIONS TO SAY WITH THE DYING

Lord, my God, I now willingly accept, as coming from your hand, whatever kind of death it pleases you to send me, with all its anguish, pains, and sorrows.

- Who can separate us from the love of Christ? (Rom. 8:35)

- If we live, we live for the Lord, and if we die, we die for the Lord. (Rom. 14: 8)

- The Lord is my light and my salvation (Ps. 27).

- I thirst for God, for the God who gives me life (Ps. 42).

- My soul thirsts for the living God (Ps. 25).

- Lord my God, I lift up my soul to You, I trust in You (Ps. 25).

- In my Father's house are many mansions (Jn. 14:2).

- I will that where I am, there ye be also with me, saith Jesus (Jn. 17:24).

- Jesus, Joseph, and Mary assist me in my agony.

2.- PSALM READING

Then, one of those present read Psalm 23:

R. The Lord is my shepherd, there is nothing I shall want.

The Lord is my shepherd, I shall not want,

He maketh me to lie down in green pastures

He leadeth me beside the still waters.

He strengthens my soul, he leads me in the path of goodness,

For his name's sake.

Though I walk through the darkest ravines

I fear no evil, for Thou art with me,

Thy rod and thy staff, they comfort me.

You serve me at table before my adversaries,

Thou anointest my head with oils

and fill my cup.

Thy goodness and thy favor are with me

my dwelling place will be the house of the Lord for a long, long time.

for a long, long time.

3.- GOSPEL: Who leads reads John 6: 37-40

A reading from the Holy Gospel according to John +

Jesus says: "All that the Father has given me will come to me, and I will not refuse him who comes to me, for I have come down from heaven, not to do my own will, but the will of him who sent me. And the will of him who sent me is that I should lose nothing of what he has given me, but that I should raise it up on the last day. My Father's will is that every man who sees the Son and believes in Him shall have eternal life: and I will raise him up at the last day."

Priest: The Gospel of the Lord.

All: Praise to you Lord Jesus Christ.

4.- LITANIES OF THE SAINTS

When the condition of the sick person could support a longer prayer, it is recommended that those present recite the litanies of the saints.

D.- Lord, have mercy	**All:** Lord, have mercy
Christ, have mercy	Christ, have mercy
Lord, have mercy	Lord, have mercy
Holy Mary, Mother of God,	**Pray for him/her**

Holy Mother of God,

St. Michael,

St. Gabriel,

Saint Raphael,

all the holy angels and archangels of God,

Abraham, our father in faith,

David, leader of God's people,

All the holy patriarchs and prophets,

St. John the Baptist,

St. Joseph,

St. Peter and St. Paul,

St. Andrew,

St. John,

St. Mary Magdalene,

St. Stephen,

St. Ignatius of Antioch,

St. Lawrence,

Saints Perpetua and Felicitas,

St. Agnes,

St. Gregory,

St. Augustine,

St. Athanasius,

St. Basil,

St. Martin,

St. Benedict,

St. Francis and St. Dominic,

St. Francis Xavier,

St. John Mary Vianney,

St. Catherine,

St. Teresa of Jesus,

Saint Toribio,

St. Rose of Lima,

St. Martin de Porres,

St. Joseph,

(Other saints can be included here...)

Saints and saints of God,

Show Yourself propitious,   **Free him/her, Lord**

From all evil,

From all sin,

From the power of Satan,

At the moment of your death,

From everlasting death,

At the day of judgment,

By thy Incarnation,

By thy sufferings and thy Cross,

By thy death and resurrection,

By the gift of the Holy Spirit,

By thy new and glorious coming,

We who are sinners,   **We beg you, hear us**

Christ, have mercy,   **Christ, have mercy**

Lead .... to eternal life,

which you promised in baptism **We beg you, hear us**

Raise him (her) up on the last day, for he (she) ate the bread of life,

Make .... share your glory, for he (she) has shared your sufferings and your death,

Jesus, Son of the living God, **We beg you, hear us**

Christ, hear us,   **Christ, hear us**

Lord Jesus, listen   **Lord Jesus, listen**

to our prayer,   **to our prayer**

5.- AT THE MOMENT OF DEATH. PRAY:

1. Christian soul, as you leave this world, march in the name of God the Father almighty, who created you; in the name of Jesus Christ, Son of the living God, who died for you; in the name of the Holy Spirit, who descended upon you. Enter into the place of peace and may your dwelling place be with God in Zion, the holy city, with the Virgin Mary, Mother of God, with St. Joseph and all the angels and saints.
R. Amen.
2. My brother or sister, I place you in the hands of Almighty God so that you may return to the same God who created you and formed you from the dust of the earth.

When you leave this world, may the Blessed Virgin Mary, the angels, and all the saints come to meet you. May our Lord Jesus Christ, who willed to die for you on the Cross, deliver you from eternal death.

May the Son of the living God bring you into his Kingdom and recognize you among his sheep, the good shepherd; may he forgive your sins and count you among his chosen ones; may you see your redeemer face to face and enjoy the contemplation of God forever and ever.

R. Amen.

V. Give, Lord, to your child the eternal salvation that awaits your mercy.

R. Amen.

V. Save, Lord, your child from all tribulations.

R. Amen.

V. Save your child, O Lord, as you saved Noah from the flood.

R. Amen.

V. Save your child, O Lord, as you saved Abraham from his enemies.

R. Amen.

V. Save your child, O Lord, as you saved Job from his sufferings.

R. Amen.

V. Save your child, O Lord, as you saved Moses from the power of Pharaoh.

R. Amen.

V. Save your child, O Lord, as you saved Daniel from the lion's den.

R. Amen.

V. Save your child, O Lord, as you saved the three young men from the fiery furnace and from the power of an unrighteous king.

R. Amen.

V. Save your child, Lord, as you saved Susanna from slander.

R. Amen.

V. Save, Lord, your son or daughter, as you saved David from the hands of Goliath and from the persecution of King Saul.

R. Amen.

V. Save, Lord, your child, as you saved Peter and Paul from prison.

R. Amen.

V. Through Jesus Christ, our Savior, who suffered such a bitter death for us and merited for us eternal life, save this child of yours, O Lord.

R. Amen.

- Finally, we can pray the **Rosary**.

6.- AT THE MOMENT THEY HAVE ALREADY DIED

When the prayers of the soul's commendation are finished, while the dying person is struggling with death, the sign of the Cross may be traced on his forehead and a crucifix may be offered to him to kiss, saying:

V. May the Father, the Son and the Holy Spirit be with you, infuse you with hope and lead you to the peace of his kingdom.

R. Amen.

When the dying person has given his soul to God, when closing his eyes, one of the relatives can say:

V. Grant, Lord, to our brother or sister ...., whose eyes will no longer see the light of this world, to contemplate eternally your beauty and to enjoy your presence forever and ever.

R. Amen.

7.- PRAYER AT THE CORPSE

This world has definitely passed away for our brother or sister...Let us ask the Lord to grant him to enjoy now the new heaven and the new earth that he has prepared for his chosen ones.

V. Come to their aid, you saints of God; go out to meet them, you angels of the Lord.

R. Receive their soul and present it before the Most High.

V. May Christ, who called you, receive you, and may the angels lead you to Abraham's bosom.

R. Receive their soul and present it before the Most High.

V. Eternal rest grant unto them, O Lord, and let perpetual light shine upon them.

R. Receive their soul and present it before the Most High.

- Then, the following prayer is said:

Let us pray. We entrust to you, Lord, your son (a) ...., so that, already dead to the world, he may live for you. With your infinite mercy, forgive the sins that human frailty has caused him/her to commit. Through Christ, our Lord.
R. Amen.

(16) <u>CELEBRATION OF CHRISTIAN DEATH</u>
PRAYERS FOR THE DECEASED

Once the dying person has passed away, the time between his death and the celebration of the funeral should be a time of charitable, friendly presence and Christian hope with those who mourn the deceased. (Recommend to the relatives that no liquor be served to those accompanying)

<u>STEP 1: COMMUNITY VIGIL FOR THE DECEASED</u>

When the house is being watched over, the body of the deceased and accompanying the family as a sign of condolence, the catechist or any of the faithful leads the following prayers:

D. Brothers, we sing: I will walk...

D. In the name of the Father, and of the Son, and of the Holy Spirit.

R.- Amen.

D. The Lord be with you.

R.- And with your spirit.

D. Brothers: Your pain is logical, for it always hurts to be separated from those we love. But at this moment, let us have confidence in the Lord, who says to us, "Come to Me all you who are weary and burdened, and I will relieve you." Therefore, let us listen to his word of comfort and pray with the confidence of the children of God.

Responsorial Psalm: Psalm 120

R.- Help comes to me from the Lord.

I lift up my eyes to the mountains; from where will help come to me? Help comes to me from the Lord who made heaven and earth.

He will not allow your foot to slip; your guardian does not slumber, the guardian of Israel neither slumbers nor rests.

The Lord keeps you in his shadow; the sun shall not hurt you by day, nor the moon by night.

The Lord preserves you from all evil, he preserves your soul, the Lord preserves your coming and going, now and forever.

Prayer: God of mercy and love, we place our brother or sister .... in your loving hands In this life You have shown him Your great love; and now that he is free from all worries, grant him eternal happiness and peace. His earthly life is now ended; receive him now in paradise, where there will be no more pains, tears or sorrows, but only peace and joy with Jesus, your Son, and the Holy Spirit, forever.

R. Amen.

D.- Let us sing: To you I lift up my eyes.

Gospel: (Jn. 12: 23-26)

D. Reading of the Holy Gospel according to St. John.

At that time Jesus said to his disciples, The hour has come for the Son of man to be glorified. Truly I tell you, unless a grain of wheat falls into the ground and dies, it remains unfruitful; but if it dies, it bears much fruit. He who loves himself loses himself, and he who hates himself in this world will keep himself for eternal life. Whoever will serve me, let him follow me; and where I am, there will my servant be also; whoever serves me, the Father will reward him.

Priest: The Gospel of the Lord.

All: Praise to you Lord Jesus Christ.

Note: A brief commentary can be made on what the Biblical text wants to tell us.

<u>OTHER READINGS FROM THE HOLY BIBLE</u>

<u>READINGS FOR A CHILD</u>

Jesus in the temple	**Luke 2: 42-52**
The humble will find relief in Jesus	**Matthew 11: 25-30**

<u>READINGS FOR YOUNG PEOPLE</u>

Jesus raises a widow's son to life	**Luke 7: 11-17**
Jesus raises Jairus' daughter from the dead	**Luke 8: 49-56**

<u>READINGS FOR ADULTS</u>

Jesus is the resurrection and the life	**John 11: 17-27**
Resurrection of Lazarus	**John 11: 32-45**
Parable of the rich and poor Lazarus	**Luke 16: 19-31**
Death of Jesus	**Luke 23: 33-46**
The final judgment	**Matthew 25: 31-46**
We must live vigilantly	**Matthew 24: 42-51**

Litany: If it seems appropriate, one of those present can lead the recitation of a short form of the litany to the saints.

At the end the following prayer may be added:

Let us pray: Lord God of mercy, hear our prayers and have mercy on your child whom you have called out of this life. Receive him or her, together with all your saints, into your kingdom of light and peace. We ask this through Christ our Lord.

R.- Amen.

Final Preces

D.- Let us pray for our brother (a) to Jesus Christ, who has said, *"I am; the resurrection and the life; he that believeth in me, though he were dead, yet shall he live, and he that is alive and believeth in me shall never die."*

D.- Lord, You who wept at the tomb of Lazarus, grant that our tears may be wiped away. **Let us pray to the Lord.**

R.- We ask you, Lord.

D.- You who raised the dead, deign to give eternal life to our brother or sister. **Let us pray to the Lord.**

D.- You who forgave the good thief on the cross and promised him paradise, deign to forgive and take our brother or sister to heaven. **Let us pray to the Lord.**

D.- You who have purified our brother or sister in the water of Baptism and anointed him or her with the oil of Confirmation, deign to admit him or her among your saints and chosen ones. **Let us pray to the Lord.**

D.- You who nourished our brother or sister with your Body and Blood, deign also to admit him or her to the table of your Kingdom. **Let us pray to the Lord.**

D.- And to us, who mourn his death, deign to comfort us with faith and the hope of eternal life. **Let us pray to the Lord.**

D.- Let us end our prayer by repeating the prayer that the Lord taught us:

R.- Our Father in heaven...

D.- Eternal rest grant unto them, O Lord.

R.- Let perpetual light shine for them.

D.- The Lord be with you.

R.- And with your spirit.

D.- May the Lord bless us, + keep us from all evil, and lead us to eternal life.

R.- Amen.

(If available, holy water is sprinkled on those present.)

D.- We sing: He is risen...

- Praying the Rosary...

<u>STEP 2: PROCESSION TO THE CHURCH</u>

When the corpse is to be taken to the church, chapel, or pantheon, the following psalm is recited:

R.- Eternal rest grant unto them, O Lord, and let perpetual light shine upon them.

Mercy, my God, by your goodness, by your immense compassion, erase my guilt. Wash away my crime, cleanse me from my sin.

R.-

For I acknowledge my guilt, I am ever mindful of my sin, against you, against you alone I sinned, I committed the wickedness you abhor.

R.-

Penitential songs are sung such as Caminaré, perdona a tu pueblo, a ti levanto mi alma, resucitó...

<u>STEP 3: AT THE CHURCH</u>

If there is no Funeral Mass, the following Response may be made:

RESPONSE

D.- Sing: Forgive your people, Lord...

D.- Do not remember my sins, O Lord.

R.- When you come to judge the world by fire.

D.- Lord, my God, direct my steps in your presence.

R.- When you come to judge the world by fire.

D.- Eternal rest grant unto them, O Lord, and let perpetual light shine upon them.

R.- When you come to judge the world by fire.

D.- Lord, have mercy.

R.- Christ, have mercy. Lord, have mercy.

D.- Our Father, lead us not into temptation.

R.- And free us from evil.

D.- From the power of hell.

R.- Free Lord, their soul.

D.- Rest in peace.

R.- **Amen.**

D.- Lord, hear my prayer.

R.- And let my cry come to You.

D.- The Lord be with you.

R.- And with your spirit.

D.- Let us pray. Absolve, we beseech thee, O Lord, the soul(s) of thy servant(s) from every bond of sin, that, in the glory of the resurrection, they may rest, risen among thy saints and elect. Through Christ our Lord.
R.- Amen.

PRAYERS

For All the Faithful Departed

Let us pray. O God, Creator and Redeemer of all the faithful, grant to the souls of your servants and handmaids the remission of all their sins so that, through our fervent supplications, they may obtain the forgiveness they have always desired. Through Christ our Lord.
R.- Amen.

For the Deceased Fathers, Let us pray

O God, who has commanded us to honor our parents, be merciful and compassionate to their souls, forgive them their sins, and give us the joy of seeing them in the joy of eternal light. Through Christ our Lord.
R.- Amen.

For Deceased Brothers, Relatives and Benefactors

O God, who grants forgiveness and lovingly seeks the salvation of mankind, we ask your clemency, through the intercession of the Blessed Virgin Mary and all the saints, to grant the grace of eternal life to the souls of our brothers and sisters, relatives and benefactors who have departed from this world. Through Christ our Lord.

R.- Amen.

On the Anniversary of the Death

O God, God of forgiveness, grant to the soul of your servant N., whose death anniversary we commemorate, the abode of peace, the rest of bliss, and the splendor of your light. Through Christ our Lord.

R.- Amen.

V.- Eternal rest grant unto them, O Lord.

R.- And let perpetual light shine for them.

V.- May they rest in peace.

R.- Amen.

V.- May their soul and those of all the faithful departed, by the mercy of God, rest in peace.

R.- Amen.

STEP 4: PRAYERS AT THE CEMETERY AND BLESSING OF THE SEPULCHER

Blessing of the Sepulcher

If the tomb is not blessed, it is blessed before the body is placed in it.

Let us pray: Lord Jesus Christ, You remained three days in the tomb, thus giving to every burial a character of waiting in the hope of the resurrection. Deign to bless this tomb and grant Your servant (a) to rest in the peace of this sepulcher until You, resurrection and life of men, resurrect him (a) and bring him (a) to contemplate the light of Your face. Thou who livest and reignest forever and ever.

R.- Amen.

(After the prayer, if there is the custom, the priest sprinkles holy water and incenses the tomb and the body of the deceased unless it is done within the rite of the last commendation).

Rite of Inhumation

The act of burying the deceased is done immediately or at the end of the rite, according to the custom of the place. While placing the body in the sepulcher, or at another opportune moment, the priest may say:

Almighty God has called our (a) brother (a), and we now bury his (her) body, that he (she) may return to the earth from whence he (she) was taken. With faith in the resurrection of Christ, the Firstborn from the dead, we believe that He will transform our humiliated body and make it like His glorious body.

Therefore, we commend our brother or sister to the Lord, that He may raise him or her up on the last day and admit him or her into the peace of His Kingdom. (If there is any comment next to the sepulcher, keep it at this time).
End with the following prayer:

Let us pray.

Lord, have mercy on your servant, that he/she may not suffer punishment for his/her faults, for he/she desired to fulfill your will. True faith united him or her here on earth to the faithful people. May your goodness now unite him or her to the choir of angels and the elect. Through Jesus Christ our Lord.

R.- Amen.

Song: He is Risen.

STEP 5: NOVENA FOR THE BLESSED SOULS IN PURGATORY

Prayers for the nine days after death. It is prayed after the Rosary.

DAY ONE

By the sign, etc.

My Lord Jesus Christ, etc.

My Lord Jesus Christ, you want us to have the utmost delicacy of conscience and perfect holiness: we beg you to grant it to us; and to those who are purifying themselves in purgatory because they have not had it, deign to apply our suffrages and bring them soon from those pains to heaven. We ask this through the intercession of your most pure Mother and St. Joseph.

Finish with the final prayer and the response.

Closing prayer for every day:

O Mary, Mother of mercy: remember the children you have in purgatory and, presenting our suffrages and your merits to your Son, intercede so that he may forgive them their debts and bring them out of that darkness into the admirable light of his glory, where they may enjoy your most sweet sight and that of your blessed Son.

O glorious Patriarch St. Joseph, intercede with your Spouse before your Son for the souls in purgatory.

V.- Do not remember, Lord, my sins.

R.- When You come to purify the world in fire.

V.- Direct my steps, O Lord my God, to Your presence.

R.- When You come to purify the world in fire.

V.- Eternal rest grant unto them, O Lord, and let eternal light shine upon them.

R.- When You come to purify the world in fire.

Lord's Prayer.

V.- From the gate of hell.

R.- Bring out, Lord, their souls.

V.- May they rest in peace.

R.- Amen.

V.- Lord, hear my prayer.

R.- And let my cry come to you.

Let us pray. O my God, on whom it is proper to have compassion and to forgive: we beseech Thee in supplication for the souls of Thy servants whom Thou hast commanded to emigrate from this world, that Thou mayest not leave them in purgatory, but command Thy holy angels to take them and bring them to the homeland of paradise, so that, since they hoped and believed in Thee, they may not suffer the pains of purgatory, but may possess eternal joys. Through Christ our Lord. Amen.

V.- Eternal rest grant unto them, O Lord.

R.- And let perpetual light shine for them.

V.- May they rest in peace.

R.- Amen.

DAY TWO

By the sign, etc.

My Lord Jesus Christ, etc.

My Lord Jesus Christ, you are the head of all your faithful Christians who are united in you as members of the one body which is the Church: we beseech you to unite us more and more with you and that our prayers and suffrages of good works may benefit the souls of our brothers and sisters in purgatory, so that they may soon be united with their brothers and sisters in heaven.

Finish with the final prayer and the response.

DAY THREE

By the sign, etc.

My Lord Jesus Christ, etc.

My Lord Jesus Christ, who punish with justice those who sin in this life or in the next: grant us the grace never to sin and have mercy on those who, having sinned, could not, for lack of time, or did not want to, for lack of will and for love of the gift, satisfy in this life and are now suffering their pains in purgatory; and to them and to all bring them soon to their rest.

Finish with the final prayer and the response.

DAY FOUR

By the sign, etc.

My Lord Jesus Christ, etc.

My Lord Jesus Christ, you demand penance even for venial sins in this world or in the next: give us a holy fear of venial sins and in mercy for those who, having committed them, are now purifying themselves in purgatory and deliver them and all sinners from their sorrows, bringing them to eternal glory.
Finish with the final prayer and the response.

DAY FIVE

By the sign, etc.

My Lord Jesus Christ, etc.

My Lord Jesus Christ, you punish in the next life those who were given away in this life, who did not pay for their guilt or did not have enough charity for the poor, with the penance that they did not do here: grant us the virtues of mortification and charity and mercifully accept our charity and suffrages, so that through them they may soon reach their eternal rest.
Finish with the final prayer and the response.

DAY SIX

By the sign, etc.

My Lord Jesus Christ, etc.

My Lord Jesus Christ, you wanted us to honor our parents and relatives and to honor our friends: we pray to you for all the souls in purgatory, but especially for the parents, relatives and friends of those of us who make this novena, so that they may attain eternal rest.
Finish with the final prayer and the response.

DAY SEVEN

By the sign, etc.

My Lord Jesus Christ, etc.

My Lord Jesus Christ, you purify in purgatory those who do not prepare themselves in time for death by receiving the last sacraments well and purifying themselves of the residues of their past evil life with terrible torments: we beseech you, Lord, for those who died unprepared and for all the others, begging you to grant them all glory and us to receive the last sacraments well.

Finish with the *final prayer and the response.*

DAY EIGHT

By the sign, etc.

My Lord Jesus Christ, etc.

My Lord Jesus Christ, you keep those who have lived in this world too fond of earthly goods and forgetful of glory from the prize, so that they may purify themselves from their negligence in desiring it: calm, merciful Lord, their anxieties and fulfill their desires, so that they may soon enjoy your presence, and grant us to love heavenly goods in such a way that we may not desire earthly goods in an inordinate way.

Finish with the *final prayer and the response.*

DAY NINE

By the sign, etc.

My Lord Jesus Christ, etc.

My Lord Jesus Christ, whose merits are infinite and whose goodness is immense: look propitiously upon your children who groan in purgatory longing for the hour to see your face, to receive your embrace, to rest at your side and; looking upon them, have pity on their sorrows and forgive what they lack to pay for their faults. We offer you our works and suffrages, those of your Saints and Saints; those of your Mother and your merits; grant that they may soon be released from their prison and receive from your hands their freedom and eternal glory. *Finish with the* *final prayer and the response.*

180

(17) BLESSINGS

<u>BLESSINGS FOR WHEN SOMEONE</u>

<u>IS GOING TO TRAVEL</u>

1.- Let us pray: Through the intercession of the Virgin Mary, may God's blessing accompany us on our journey in union with our guardian angel. Amen. Saint Mary of the Way, pray for us. Saint Raphael, pray for us.

2.- Let us pray: God bless us with all kinds of heavenly blessings and happily dispose our paths so that we may always experience his divine protection in this journey we are about to undertake. Amen. St. Mary of the Way, pray for us. Saint Raphael, pray for us.

<u>WHEN A NEW HOUSE IS INAUGURATED</u>

Catechist: We pray together as brothers.

C.- In the name of the Father, and of the Son, and of the Holy Spirit.

R.- Amen.

C.- The peace of the Lord be with this house and all who dwell here.

R.- And with your spirit.

C.- Brothers, let us direct our fervent prayer to Jesus Christ, who willed to be born of the Virgin Mary and dwell among us so that He may deign to enter this house and bless it with his presence.

Now let us listen to the Holy Gospel according to Luke (Lk. 10: 5-9). Jesus said to His disciples:

When you enter a house, first say, 'Peace to this house.' And if there are people of peace there, your peace will rest on them; if not, it will return to you. Stay in the same house; eat and drink of what they have, for the laborer deserves his wages. Do not move from house to house. If you enter a town and it receives you well, eat what you put on, cure the sick who are there, and say, The kingdom of God is at hand for you.

The Gospel of the Lord.

R.- Praise to you, Lord Jesus Christ.

C.- Now, let us call upon our God with the petitions. We answer: Stay with us, Lord.

1. Abide in our home, Lord, so that we may worship and glorify you all our lives. Let us pray to the Lord.

2. You, who are the head of the Church, who cares and loves her, let each of the members of this family help the happiness of others and keep away quarrels and grudges. Let us pray to the Lord.

3. Lord, help the family that will inhabit this house so that among them, there may be communication dialogue and allow them to live in peace.

<u>(18) RELIGIOUS FESTIVALS</u>

<u>JANUARY</u>
1.   Holy Mary, Mother of God
6.   Epiphany
17.   St. Anthony Abbot
24.   St. Francis de Sales
25.   Conversion of St. Paul
26.   Saints Timothy and Titus
28.   St. Thomas Aquinas
31.   St. John Bosco

<u>FEBRUARY</u>
2.   Presentation of the Lord
6.   St. Paul Miky and Companions Martyrs
10.   St. Jose Luis Sanchez del Rio
11.   Our Lady of Lourdes
22.   St. Peter's Chair

<u>MARCH</u>
19.   St. Joseph
25.   The Annunciation

<u>APRIL</u>
25.   St. Mark
27.   St. Toribio of Mogrovejo
30.   St. Pius V.

<u>MAY</u>
1.   St. Joseph the Worker
2.   St. Athanasius
3.   Veneration of the Holy Cross
4.   Apostles Philip and James
13.   Our Lady of Fatima
14.   Saint Matthias
15.   St. Isidore Labrador
24.   Mary Help of Christians
31.   The Visitation

<u>JUNE</u>
13.   St. Anthony of Padua
21.   St. Aloysius Gonzaga
22.   St. Thomas More
24.   St. John the Baptist
26.   St. Josemaría Escrivá
27.   Our Lady of Perpetual Help
29.   Holy Apostles Peter and Paul
Friday after Corpus Christi: Sacred Heart of Jesus and on Saturday: Immaculate Heart of Mary.

JULY

3.	St. Thomas the Apostle
4.	St. Elizabeth of Portugal
6.	St. Maria Goretti
10.	St. Christopher
11.	St. Benedict
15.	St. Bonaventure
16.	Our Lady of Mount Carmel
22.	St. Mary Magdalene
25.	St. James the Greater
26.	St. Joachim and St. Anne
29.	Saint Martha
31.	St. Ignatius of Loyola

AUGUST

1.	St. Alphonsus Ma. de Liguori
2.	Our Lady of the Angels
4.	St. John Mary Vianney
6.	Transfiguration of the Lord
8.	St. Dominic of Guzman
10.	St. Lawrence
14.	St. Maximilian Kolbe
15.	The Assumption of the Virgin
21.	St. Pius X
22.	St. Mary, Queen
St.	Bartholomew
28.	St. Augustine
30.	St. Rose of Lima

SEPTEMBER

1.	The Nativity of Our Lady
14.	Exaltation of the Most Holy Cross
15.	The Sorrows of Our Lady
18.	St. John Macias
21.	St. Matthew
24.	The Mercy
28.	Lord of the Side
29.	Holy Archangels Gabriel, Michael and Rafae l

OCTOBER

1.	Saint Therese of the Child Jesus
2.	Guardian Angels
4.	St. Francis of Assisi
7.	Our Lady of the Rosary
12.	Our Lady of the Pillar
15.	Saint Theresa of Jesus
18.	Saint Luke
21.	Blessed Charles of Austria

24.   St. Anthony Mary Claret
28.   Lord of Miracles
29.   Saints Simon and Jude Thaddeus

<u>NOVEMBER</u>
1.   All Saints
2.   All Souls Day
3.   St. Martin de Porres
4.   St. Charles Borromeo
17.   St. Elizabeth of Hungary
21.   Presentation of the Virgin
22.   St. Cecilia
27.   Our Lady of the Miraculous Medal
30.   St. Andrew

<u>DECEMBER</u>
3.   St. Francis Xavier
6.   St. Nicholas
7.   St. Ambrose
8.   Immaculate Conception
12.   Our Lady of Guadalupe
13.   Saint Lucia
14.   St. John of the Cross
25.   Christmas
26.   St. Stephen
27.   St. John the Evangelist
28.   Holy Innocents

(19) WHY AM I CATHOLIC?

I am Catholic because I know that the Catholic Church was founded by Jesus of Nazareth in 33 A.D. and that Christ is alive within His Church. Jesus founded the Catholic Church and appointed St. Peter, the first leader of His Church, known as the Pope.

And I say to you that you are Peter, and on this rock I will build my church. (Matthew 16:18)

We meet Christ face to face in the 7 Sacraments that He Himself founded and instituted for our benefit, and that evidence of this is in the millions of miracles that He has worked through many saints over the last two thousand years and in the many Eucharistic miracles that have occurred over the centuries.

(20) <u>PRAYER TO SAINT MICHAEL THE ARCHANGEL</u>

St. Michael the Archangel, defend us in battle; be our protection against the wickedness and snares of the devil. May God rebuke him, we humbly pray.

And do, though, prince of the heavenly militia, with the divine power that God has granted you, cast into hell Satan and the other evil spirits that are scattered throughout the world seeking the perdition of souls.

Amen.

<u>(21) MY LIFE OF BLESSINGS</u>

<u>LIST OF 7 WAYS GOD HAS BLESSED ME IN MY LIFE:</u>

1.

2.

3.

4.

5.

6.
7.

<u>LIST OF 7 WAYS I CAN RETURN MY BLESSINGS TO OTHERS IN MY LIFE:</u>

1.

2.

3.

4.

5.

6.

7.

<u>(22) CATHOLIC RESOURCES ON THE WEB</u>

Find Your Parish and Mass Times:
https://catholicmasstime.org/church/search

Formed.org

The Holy See/Vatican:
https://www.vatican.va/content/vatican/en.html

U.S. Conference of Catholic Bishops:
https://www.usccb.org/about

The Diocese of Arlington, Virginia:
https://www.arlingtondiocese.org

(23) THE HOLY BOOKS OF THE BIBLE

Old Testament

- Genesis (Gen)
- Exodus (Ex)
- Leviticus (Lv)
- Numbers (Num)
- Deuteronomy. (Dt)
- Joshua (Jos)
- Judges (Jg)
- Ruth (Ru)
- 1 Samuel. (1 Sam)
- 2 Samuel. (2 Sam)
- 1 Kings (1 Kg)
- 2 Kings (2 Kg)
- 1 Chronicles (1 Chr)
- 2 Chronicles (2 Chr)
- Ezra (Ezra)
- Nehemiah (Neh)
- Tobit (Tb)
- Judith (Jdt)
- Esther (Est)
- Job (Job)
- Psalms (Ps)
- 1 Maccabees (1 Mac)
- 2 Maccabees (2 Mac)
- Proverbs (Pr)
- Qohelet. (Ecclesiastes) (Qo or Eccl)
- Song of Solomon (S of S)
- Wisdom (Wis)
- Jeremiah (Jer)
- Lamentations (Lm)
- Sirach (Ecclesiasticus) (Sir)
- Isaiah (Is)
- Ezekiel (Ezec)
- Daniel (Dan)

- Hosea (Hos)
- Joel (Jl)
- Baruch (Ba)
- Amos (Am)
- Obadiah (Abd)
- Jonah (Jon)
- Micah (Mic)
- Nahum (Nah)
- Habakkuk (Hab)
- Zephaniah (Zeph)
- Haggai (Hag)
- Zechariah (Zech)
- Malachi (Mal)

New Testament

- Matthew (Mt.)
- Mark (Mr. or Mk.)
- Luke (Lk.)
- John (Jn.)
- Acts (Acts)
- Romans (Rom.)
- 1 Corinthians (1 Cor)
- 2 Corinthians (2 Cor)
- Galatians (Gal.)
- Ephesians (Eph.)
- Philippians. (Phil.)
- Colossians. (Col.)
- 1 Thessalonians. (1 Thess.)
- 2 Thessalonians. (2 Thess.)
- 1 Timothy (1 Tim.)
- 2 Timothy (2 Tim.)
- Titus (Titus)
- Philemon (Phlm.)
- Hebrews (Heb.)
- James (Jas.)
- 1 Peter (1 Pet. or 1 Pe.)

- 2 Peter (2 Pet. or 2 Pe.)
- 1 John (1 Jn.)
- 2 John (2 Jn.)
- 3 John (3 Jn.)
- Jude (Jud. or Jds.)
- Revelation (Rev.)

THE CATHOLIC CHURCH IS YOUR HOME IN EVERY COUNTRY OF THE WORLD!

Use this website to find your local Catholic parish in the United States, go there, attend mass and get involved:

catholicmasstime.org

THE PARISH IS MY HOME

I belong to the Diocese of:_________________________________

My Bishop's name is:_________________________________

My Parish is called:_________________________________

The priests are called:_________________________________

I was baptized on:__________________/__________________/ 20

Together, we can build God's Kingdom of Heaven!

In Order to Buy More Copies of this Catechism, Please Visit: andrewjheintz.com or amazon.com

www.ingramcontent.com/pod-product-compliance
Lightning Source LLC
Chambersburg PA
CBHW040138160726
48006CB00014B/1541